KV-637-873

Fast build

Edited by Dennis Stacey

UNIVERSITY OF WOLVERHAMPTON
LIBRARY

Acc No.

CLASS

CONTROL
0727716212

692

FAS

DATE
12 DEC 1995

SITE
RS

GIFT

Thomas Telford, London

This book is based on papers presented at the conference *Fast build from trade contractor to client: building into the 21st century from the 20th century*, which was organized by the Institution of Civil Engineers, co-sponsored by the Institution of Mechanical Engineers, the Royal Institute of British Architects and the Chartered Institute of Building, and held at the Brewery, Chiswell Street, London, on 10 May 1990.

Published by Thomas Telford Ltd, Thomas Telford House, 1 Heron Quay, London E14 4JD

First published 1991

Conversion factor
1 ft^2 0·0929 m^2

British Library Cataloguing in Publication Data
Fast build.
  I. Stacey, D.
  692

ISBN: 0 7277 1621 2

© Authors, 1991

All rights, including translation reserved. Except for fair copying, no part of this publication may be reproduced, stored in a retrieval system or transmitted in any form or by any means, electronic, mechanical, photocopying or otherwise, without the prior written permission of the Publications Manager, Publications Division, Thomas Telford Ltd, Thomas Telford House, 1 Heron Quay, London E14 4JD.

The book is published on the understanding that the authors are solely responsible for the statements made and opinions expressed in it and that its publication does not necessarily imply that such statements and or opinions are or reflect the views or opinions of the publishers.

Typeset in Great Britain by MHL Typesetting Limited, Coventry.
Printed and bound in Great Britain by
Butler & Tanner Ltd, Frome and London

Contents

Introduction

D. STACEY, Bovis Construction Ltd

Fast build is not programme chasing where cost control is lost in the pursuit of time achievement. Quite often programme chasing (or fast track) will fail because the key components to building fast are just not there. What is worse is that the people involved do not realize that these vital ingredients are missing. Fast build is the achieving of the quickest possible construction time without any sacrifice in quality and cost.

The building industry has been doing things in much the same way for a long time. Time and cost overruns are endemic and clients are dissatisfied with the performance of the industry. They do not want the initial estimate to be half the final cost and the completion date to be missed.

Fast build demands a raising of standards from all those involved in the industry. It breaks down cultural barriers which stand in the way of progress to a more professional and competent industry. Clients have seen shining examples in the gloom of mediocrity and are asking why it is that the best examples are not normal practice.

The projects described in this book — a purpose-built office block of an insurance company, headquarters for the RAF Support Command and multiphase office development in the City of London for a major property company — have recurring themes.

The clients could not have been more different but they all wanted a quality project to time and cost parameters which were outside the usual industry achievement rates. In other words they were looking for fast build. These clients set about achieving their goals with different forms of contract: two-stage tender, design and build, and construction management. However, it appears that whatever the contract, providing it is not actually obstructive, it is not a major factor in fast build. What is essential is for the will, skill and intent applied to achieving a common objective to be present in the building team.

In all the examples presented teamwork was much in evidence: the client, professionals and construction team joined together to follow an agreed path to a common objective. In particular the subcontractor (trade contractor) was recognized as the expert in his particular speciality, and this was to the benefit of all the parties involved. In the UK construction industry the skills of subcontractor are rarely enjoyed to the full by any client.

Clear client objectives with a well thought out route to achieve those goals were also much in evidence. Being enthusiastic is not enough: objectives and the means of achieving them must be clear. The ability to be flexible in the approach to contractual matters helped to avoid sources of conflict. Clients and professionals were willing to set aside the enshrined dogma of decades and try a more imaginative response to the needs of the projects.

All the projects brought together those in the construction process on a non-confrontational basis. The result of this pooling of effort and skill is probably the most striking feature of these fast-build projects. It made it possible for everyone involved at all levels to question in a constructive way, and offer useful advice to the betterment of the task in hand. This helped to generate the right attitude and, in no small way, raised the status of those involved. In particular, the subcontractor was able to contribute directly to the design and co-ordination of the project.

For the commercial office development it was important that the construction manager was the focal point in the decision-making. However, common to all projects was the importance of clear definition of responsibilities, particularly in respect of design. Confusion over who is responsible for designing what and by when is probably the biggest single source of time and cost overrun in the industry. What has been recognized is the need to manage the design process so that the required information emerges when it is wanted.

For all the projects, the building team members were carefully selected. The subcontractors were selected after careful screening not only for their technical capacity but also for a stand-alone and positive attitude. The proper level of management was sought from the director through to the site foreman. Conditions were created in which the subcontractors could operate at the highest level of output through properly organized sites with good communications and proper meeting structures. Decision-makers were present at all meetings, from those where the day's objectives were reviewed right up to regular directors' meetings. Good welfare facilities were provided and subcontractors were encouraged to communicate with their work-force.

The talents of the parties involved must be recognized and then a structure created whereby the participants are left to do what they are best at doing: the designer to design, the construction manager (or contractor) to organize the building works and the subcontractor to construct.

Achievement should be rewarded on a regular basis. Reward can be for a whole range of matters from a good safety record to quality control. At all times people must be recognized and the environment created for people and organizations to succeed.

The papers also have common themes on the actual construction process. Some important construction points were adopted and some (for instance, as noted in the introspective analysis of the trade contractors working on the Broadgate project) were recognized as missing.

Above all standardization and simplicity are important. So often in the UK standardization of design and components is considered to stifle good design. This is not so. Why should the architrave width on the fifth floor be different from that on the fourth floor? Does it really matter whether the construction gap betewen the concrete frame and the exterior cladding is 6 mm or 46 mm? It is not seen and never will be, but the difference in time and cost in constructing to such demanding but irrelevant tolerances is colossal.

Good design is not compromised by standardization or simplicity. Putting value where it is best appreciated is a newly emerging skill which makes it possible to decide where money should be concentrated to achieve uniqueness. Non-standardization does not automatically mean good design. Subcontractors appreciate details that are familiar and work gets done more quickly when people know what they are doing.

Projects should be designed and engineered on paper before construction starts. It is a lot cheaper to correct mistakes at the drawing-board stage. Fast build cannot be achieved without properly thought through design.

The environment of building sites is hostile to the assembly of engineered components. Obviously some activities have to take place on site. On all of the projects described effort was made to prefabricate as much as possible in the more friendly environment of a factory.

Getting quality right first time and preferably off site has captured the attention of the contributors to this book. Correcting quality problems after components have been installed on site is costly, time-consuming and an anathema to the concept of fast build.

Building should be constructed to a watertight stage as quickly as possible even if that means there have to be temporary enclosures. Factory conditions need to be created on site as soon as is possible.

There is no one simple way to fast build. It is an attitude and an ethos. It needs to be believed in and made to work by everyone involved in the building industry.

Skandia Life headquarters building, Southampton

Design

A. A. LETT, Director, Aukett Associates

The Skandia project is located prominently in Southampton opposite the Civic Centre, on the slope of the old coastal escarpment. It is an eleven-storey structure, providing 100 000 ft^2 net offices and 162 car spaces. The section takes advantage of the natural slope, with all parking cut into the slope, forming the first three levels, and all office accommodation from level 4 upwards.

The office space is a simple U shape around an atrium. The atrium opens to the town and Civic Centre spaces, while the offices take advantage of the superb views over the docks and River Test.

The atrium is bridged at each level, by a deck providing access to the wall-climber lifts and core accommodation. There are four lifts in all, two wall climbers and two general purpose lifts which also fulfil goods and fire-fighting functions. There are therefore four cores at each level, servicing approximately 12 000 – 15 000 ft^2 net per floor.

Apart from disabled car users, all entry to the building is channelled into the atrium, under a large steel canopy structure which forms a focus to the atrium frontage.

The structure is based on a 7·5 m square grid to suit car parking, with one central column omitted to provide a larger multi-purpose space per floor. This is located behind the glass bay on the west elevation.

The foundation is a deep raft; the car park is of reinforced concrete construction, while office accommodation above is a steel frame, with Holorib concrete floors and a lightweight prefabricated cladding. The building is air-conditioned, using fan coils located in the ceiling zone, with floor servicing via a 200 mm deep raised floor.

Architectural decisions

When the structural principles for the building had been established, there were a number of architectural issues which were influenced and constrained by these decisions.

The shape and form of the building were established at an early stage. There were, however, no preconceptions about cladding materials, other than that they should be prefabricated off site to allow rapid enclosure of the envelope, to achieve as early a watertight construction as possible. In fact, the requirements for accommodation of structural movement from the raft eliminated many of the options and led to the development of a lightweight cladding system, capable of accommodating both the structural movement and the severe exposure of the site. The cladding is an all-aluminium part-rainscreen system, using hung, aluminium external panels finished with syntha-pulvin, and luxguard CR20 blue glass. All aluminium components were UK-manufactured. Ceilings and floors are typical of many office buildings where speed and simplicity are essential ingredients. Walls are dry-lined plasterboard, selected to minimize wet trades and to reduce weight on the steel structure.

The principles of speed, a simple roof and enclosure to achieve an early watertight stage and 'dry' prefabricated finishes were regarded as essential ingredients of fast-build construction.

Fast build

In this project, the procurer or customer has sought a building as a 'one off' commission. The site has difficult ground conditions, and structural solutions and client priorities have largely determined the construction and contractual route.

However, irrespective of form of contract, today's buildings need to be conceived on a fast-build subcontractor-orientated approach, to allow the design and construction teams the flexibility to achieve the best balance between cost and time that the market-place will allow. The relative weighting between cost and time varies from project to project, but irrespective of form of contract, time tends to mean money.

The JCT form of contract may not be ideal. However, there is such a muddle concerning management contracting, construction management, forms of design and build, and so on, that I think the construction industry should not be too surprised to see a newcomer to the business of putting up buildings totally confused and resorting to JCT as a commonly used form. In the UK this industry does itself no credit by being unable to present a more clearly defined, easily understood set of contractual arrangements to its prospective customers.

Inadequacies of contractual methods aside, the fundamental requirement for successful fast-build projects is to harness the skills of all members of the team, including the contractor and subcontractors, to focus on the process of analysing, testing and questioning each issue in a constructive way so that decisions can be taken in an atmosphere of co-operation, without many of the traditional 'them and us' attitudes that have plagued the industry in the past.

Construction should be seen as a profession along with all the other skills, and each team member should understand his own limits, while respecting the roles of others.

This attitude, together with a real 'shake-up' of contractual options, provides the clue for building to progress from the 20th to the 21st century.

Project co-ordination and quantity surveying

H. E. PERRY, Senior Partner, Silk & Frazier

Skandia originated in Sweden; the UK side of the business commenced in London in 1979. The business grew rapidly and the main office was re-located to Southampton. The initial office suite was soon outgrown and further space was acquired in the same building. During 1986 it became apparent that Skandia would require even more space in the foreseeable future. As the break clauses in the leases for their various office suites would become operable in 2−3 years' time, the Directors considered the prospect of constructing their own building.

As Skandia's agent, Castleman and Dean were asked to find a site for the proposed new building. After several months the present site was located. It had the desired size and location; however, it did not have planning permission for a major office building.

Castleman and Dean were given a brief to assemble a team comprising an architect, a structural engineer and a quantity surveyor, whose task it would be to prepare a feasibility study so that Skandia could submit a bid for the site in early 1987. The team was selected between Christmas 1986 and the new year, and the feasibility study, complete with drawings, model, costs and report, was presented early in February 1987.

The site was purchased in June 1987 and the vendor imposed the condition that an access road should be constructed by the end of September 1988 to service the adjoining supermarket currently under construction, and that the development of the site should commence by November 1988 and proceed to completion.

As Skandia were nervous to venture into the cost commitment of a major building project and aware of their ultimate cost exposure, the company appointed Joint Project Co-ordinators to advise them and to be their link with the professional design team. As one of these co-ordinators, I had a foot in both camps as Client Representative and as Project Quantity Surveyor.

The design team for the new building was appointed in November 1987, the feasibility study having been a separate and self-contained appointment.

As the design was developed by the architect in conjunction with the engineer, the quantity surveyor prepared a series of cost plans and cost checks, and the present design (which closely resembles the initial concept) gradually evolved.

Considerable research was carried out on the foundation aspect, the options of piling and of a reinforced concrete raft being examined in detail. Eventually the raft option was adopted on the basis of cost and reduction of risk through the likelihood of obstructions being encountered during the piling operations.

Fast build

Fast build, to my mind, means not only the speed of construction on site but also the time taken in the selection and appointment of the contractor and the ascertainment of the contract sum. Table 1 shows that the design team were appointed in November 1987 and that work commenced on site in January 1989. This may not have been very quick, but Skandia, who were nervous and conscious of their anticipated cost commitment, were holding back from making the final decision to instruct the design team to proceed to tender stage. The instruction was given at the end of June 1988 on the understanding that competitive tenders were to be received and that an end figure was to be identified.

Once Skandia had given instructions to proceed, no time was to be lost in setting in motion the procedure that would satisfy

Table 1. Milestone dates

Feasibility study	
Team appointed	31.12.86
Various scheme options and model presented to Skandia directors	13.1.87
Feasibility report presented to Skandia board of directors	18.2.87
Contracts exchanged for site purchase	10.9.87
Design team appointed for new building	1.11.87
Planning application submitted	17.6.88
Planning approval granted	28.7.88
Supermarket service access road Designed, tendered and constructed	June—Oct. 1988
Cost plan approved and architects' proposals signed off	28.6.88
Tender procurement	
Bills of quantities for section 1 (substructure) and section 2 (superstructure) started	8.8.88
Tender documents sent out	14.9.88
Tenders submitted	26.10.88
Tender report to Skandia board of directors	2.11.88
Letter of intent to Ernest Ireland	22.12.88
Contract commencement date	30.1.89
Projected shell and core completion	1.8.90
Contract completion date (96 weeks)	3.12.90

the client's requirements, which were

(a) to commence development of the site in September 1988 to comply with the conditions of the sale of the site to Skandia

(b) to obtain competitive tenders to achieve a quantified and agreed contract sum

(c) to minimize Skandia's financial risks.

With a start date of September 1988 and instructions to proceed given only at the end of June, it was clear that it would be practically impossible to obtain competitive tenders for the whole scope of the works by traditional tendering on fully measured bills of quantities. At this time the architect's drawings were not far beyond the preliminary stage.

To satisfy the condition of commencing the development of the site in September 1988, the supermarket service ramp and associated retaining walls were designed, drawn and tendered for, and to this contract was added the demolition and enabling works on the main site, together with complicated diversion of high voltage mains electricity cabling. The contract was let on the JCT Minor Works Contract after competitive tenders had been invited. This work was commenced 18 July 1988 and completed early in November 1988.

The first objective was therefore achieved satisfactorily. Concurrently, the problem of how to obtain meaningful realistic competitive tenders for the main building works in the shortest possible time on the basis of the information available, or likely to be available in July 1988, was being considered.

On examination of the situation it was clear that the new building, as proposed, neatly divided itself into two distinct and differing sections. Section 1 was the underground reinforced concrete car-parking accommodation sitting on the deep reinforced concrete raft and occupying levels 1−4.

Section 2 was the remainder of the building from level 4 upwards, which was designed to have a structural steel frame, with lightweight concrete floor slabs cast on profiled metal permanent shuttering. A system of glazing and wall cladding was envisaged, both externally and for the inner walls of the atrium. The building was to be air-conditioned and finished to a speculative developer's specification. The fitting out for Skandia's own occupation was to be treated as 'tenant's extras'.

The design of section 1 was reasonably well advanced due to the fact that the engineer had gone into considerable detail on the options under consideration, namely a piled foundation and a raft foundation, to enable the quantity surveyor to carry out the financial assessment of the options. Section 2 was drawn but not detailed or specified.

After consideration and discussion it was agreed that two tenders would be invited from selected contractors. Section 1 would be tendered for on JCT 80 with firm quantities. Section 2 would be tendered for on JCT 80 with approximate quantities. The lowest tender for each section would be considered for acceptance.

The timetable for tender procurement is shown in Table 1. It can be seen that from receiving client approval for the cost plan on 28 June 1988 to receiving tenders on 26 October 1988, a period of four months elapsed. On a project of this size and complexity, this represents a saving of at least three months over the traditional route of complete architectural drawings and information and full bills of quantities.

Activities

The bills of quantities and other tender documents for section 1 were prepared as a separate self-contained contract from detailed drawings and specifications prepared by the structural engineer.

The bills of quantities for section 2 were not so traditional in view of the limited drawn information available and the preliminary stage of development. It was decided to prepare a document which

(*a*) would contain sufficient information for the tendering contractors to ascertain the scope and volume of the work involved

(*b*) would be a suitable document for obtaining realistic competitive tenders

(*c*) would provide a satisfactory basis for pricing the work ultimately designed and re-measured.

For the straightforward elements such as concrete work, blockwork and brickwork, floor, wall and ceiling finishes and external works and drainage, the measurement of the quantities was based on the preliminary sketch drawings currently available, supplemented by question and answer sheets and details of similar projects that had been completed by the architect. The more specialized elements, covered by provisional sums, were to be tendered for by specialist subcontractors, and the selected firms were to become the contractor's own domestic subcontractors, some with a 'contractor design' responsibility. As in the case of section 1, this section was documented as a self-contained contract with its own preliminaries and conditions of contract.

In the meantime a list of likely contractors was compiled by the design team and discussed with the directors of Skandia. The long list of suggested contractors was sifted and refined to a short list of five firms.

The firms were all invited to attend interviews with the design team, at which the proposed procurement strategy was explained in detail. It was also explained that during the anticipated six-month contract period for section 1, the section 2 design would be advanced and accurate bills would be prepared; these would be priced and agreed with the successful contractor at the bill rates for section 2 which were obtained by competitive tendering. Ultimately, all five contractors were included in the tender list and both section 1 and section 2 tender documents were dispatched to them.

While the contractors were preparing their tenders for the main works, drawings, specifications and tender documents were prepared for the structural steel frame, the metal decking, the mechanical and electrical services, the lifts and the external cladding. The intention was to substitute known tender sums for the provisional sums in the bills of quantities when adjudicating on the main tenders.

The bills for section 2 of the works contained a number of alternative good quality finishings so that measured rates could be obtained, so providing a 'shopping basket' of optional items to choose from and assisting in formulating the final specifications necessary to achieve the budget.

Main contractors' tenders were received on the due date and the process of adjudication commenced. It was considered sensible to award the contract to the firm that submitted the lowest aggregate for sections 1 and 2, thus avoiding the possibility of changing contractors at the completion of section 1. In the event this proved to be a good decision, for the thought of changing horses in midstream is horrific! The three lowest tenderers were fairly close in the value of their bids and in the time offered to carry out the works.

The tenders received were substantially above budget, due to the fact that many high quality finishings were included to obtain a quantified schedule of rates. A reduction of tender was prepared; the contractors submitting the lowest tenders were interviewed and the revisions were explained to them in detail. They were then invited to submit fresh tenders on the revised documentation, which included the results of the subcontract tendering for the steelwork and the mechanical and electrical installations.

After careful consideration and discussion with the Skandia Board, a letter of intent was sent to Ernest Ireland just before Christmas 1988, and the contract commencement date was agreed as 30 January 1989.

Section 1, the reinforced concrete raft and basement car parking, was of robust traditional construction and included dewatering and temporary works to uphold adjacent roads and footpaths. It was work that by its very nature could not be short-circuited or carried out in any other way. Thus, this section of the work, which represented 15% of the contract value, was going to take almost 30% of the contract period.

Section 2 therefore needed to be built very quickly, hence the choice of the steel frame with metal decking and curtain walling.

While the final details were being negotiated with Ernest Ireland, it was agreed that the project would be treated as one contract, and the intermediate remeasurement process for section 2 would be dispensed with.

As the work proceeded, each element, as and when designed, was cost-checked against the allowances in the bills of quantities, and if necessary re-designed to achieve the budget. The remainder of the elements covered by provisional sums were tendered for and monitored against the budget.

Attitudes

The process has been time-consuming for the design team but has worked due to the attitudes of the members of the design team and the main contractor. There is no doubt that the site commencement date was achieved considerably earlier than would have been the case by a more traditional approach.

However, there is no perfect solution that will cover all situations, and a process that is successful for one contract is not automatically the magic solution for all contracts. The factors which are essential are the right attitude and flexibility.

Structural engineering

D. KAYE, Project Director, Ove Arup & Partners

In terms of construction materials, the structure of the eleven-storey Skandia building divides itself into two. Up to and including level 4 is in situ reinforced concrete. Above this level, the frame is structural steel with in situ lightweight concrete floors.

The horizontal stability of the completed building is provided by four steel-braced cores. On the north and south elevations, steel beams and columns act with the cores to provide increased stiffness. Loads are transmitted to these cores and frames by the diaphragm action of the floors.

The foundation is a stepped in situ concrete raft, which also forms the level 1 car park.

Soil conditions and foundations

The site falls from east to west at a slope of approximately 1 in 10. The soils on the site are a mixture of clay and sand about 30 m deep. They are not strong enough to permit the use of separate surface foundations at each column position. Groundwater was encountered in all of the boreholes, and in the lower part of the site was close to the surface.

The possibility of using either reinforced concrete bored piles or a reinforced concrete raft was investigated. Piles may be considered the more traditional solution for a building of this size on a site with these soil conditions. They have the advantage that the loads are transferred to a deeper and stiffer soil stratum, but do add significantly to the cost and time of construction of the building.

It was agreed that the option of a raft solution should be pursued because overall the soil immediately beneath the building is strong enough to support the loads imposed on it by the building and it was estimated that it would save about £0·5 million. Also, the construction period would be about four weeks shorter than for the piled alternative.

A characteristic of the raft solution is that the deflections and movements of the building are increased. This was carefully analysed and the implications for the design of services and finishes were included in the contract documents.

Apart from the estimated saving in time and cost, a chief attraction of the raft to the client was the reduction in risk. As is often the case, the key to finishing on time is the completion to programme of works in the ground. With a difficult site to build on, it was felt that the risk of delays due to work in the ground was reduced as much as possible by using a raft rather than piles.

To enable an early site start, and to allow more time for detail development of the superstructure design, it was proposed that the construction below level 4 (contract 1) should be tendered for and built as a separate contract from the remainder of the work, with no overlap. From the point of view of geometry and change in structural materials, the project lent itself to this approach.

The contractor was allowed a period of six months to build contract 1 and this was completed to programme.

Concrete (levels 1–4)
The suspended floors are in general flat slabs without column head drops, spanning 7·5 m in two directions. In the central area the span is increased to 9 m and at level 4 there is a cantilever which varies from 2·5 m to 4 m. The edges of suspended slabs and ramps have 500 mm upstand beams, and downstand beams support a lift pit which is suspended from the level 4 slab.

Vertical loads are carried by columns which spring directly from the 1·6 m reinforced concrete raft. Stairs are in situ reinforced concrete.

The site slopes up to the east, and the raft is formed in three levels. Retaining walls along the east elevation and parts of the north and south elevations span between the raft and the level 4 slab.

The level 4 slab has holding-down assemblies cast into it, supplied by the steel fabricator for connection of the steel superstructure.

Superstructure (level 4 to roof)

The floors comprise 130 mm lightweight concrete cast in situ on profiled metal decking. The metal decking is designed to span 2·5 m between steel secondary beams to support the wet concrete unpropped and construction loading. In the permanent condition the metal decking acts as reinforcement for the lightweight concrete and supports all imposed loads, finishes and services.

The slab has additional reinforcement comprising A142 mesh with extra reinforcement where there is a need for shear transfer or to meet the requirements for fire protection.

In general, all steel floor beams are designed as simply supported, using the composite action of the concrete floor and steel beams by the inclusion of through-deck welded shear studs installed on site. Typically they span 7·5 m between beams and columns.

Stanchions are generally uncased universal column sections which carry the beam reactions direct to the foundations. The storey height is 4·15 m.

All connections were designed by the steelwork fabricator to the loads indicated on the drawings.

Temporary works

Concurrent with the preparation of the design, a sequence of construction was developed by the consulting engineer. Particular attention was paid to dewatering the site, and the temporary support of the Civic Centre road.

Both of these matters were discussed in considerable depth with the tenderers, in order that the engineer could be satisfied that sufficient thought had been given at that stage. Of particular note was the Venturi dewatering system that had been proposed.

Both prior to commencement on site and during the works, the consulting engineer continued to liaise closely with the main contractor and the specialist dewatering firm to monitor the efficiency of the system in the light of any further site data which became available.

Tendering strategy

The tendering strategy was to provide a full bill of quantities for contract 1, covering the in situ concrete work up to level 4, and essential drainage and builders' work. At the same time, a bill of approximate quantities for the remainder of the work was provided (contract 2). The contractor was selected on the basis of the two tenders submitted.

While contract 1 was being constructed, firm bills of quantities were prepared for contract 2; these were priced at the rates contained in the bills of approximate quantities and a contract sum was negotiated and agreed. (In the unlikely event of a contract sum for contract 2 not having being agreed, the contractor's involvement would have terminated on completion of contract 1.)

Significant factors

The aim was to reduce risk and so reduce the possibility of delays. This was achieved in the following ways.

(a) The foundation system with minimum risk was chosen. (Work in the ground is always the area of greatest risk, and completion on time was crucial to commencement of steelwork erection.)

(b) Temporary works were considered early, and the dewatering system was chosen carefully. The latter greatly reduced the problem of both excavation and casting concrete in difficult ground conditions.

(c) Detailed pre-tender interviews were held to ensure that contractors with the right experience were included on the tender list, and to confirm their availability and resources.

(d) Tendering was carried out in parallel for the main contract and for major subcontracts such as the steel frame, cladding, mechanical and electrical works and lifts.

(e) Early joint discussions were held with the main contractor and key subcontractors to discuss programme and method of construction.

(f) Steelwork designs were simple and member sizes were standardized.

(g) All steelwork drawings were issued at one time to allow all the steelwork to be ordered at one time.

(h) Concrete details were simple (flat slab, no drops, etc.).

The emphasis was placed on reduced risk, resulting in reduced arguments, and so leading to better all round co-operation and giving a greater likelihood of the programme being achieved.

Construction

A. WARD, Construction Director, Ernest Ireland Construction

Ernest Ireland Construction are the south and south-west operating arm of Mowlem Regional Construction Ltd.

Before the decision was taken to tender for this project, much thought had to be given regarding the availability of the special resources that would be required to undertake this imaginative form of 'fast build' contract.

To get the building under construction at the earliest possible date, the decision had been made to divide the project into two phases. This gave Ernest Ireland the opportunity of submitting a competitive bid for phase 1 on a detailed bill of quantities, along with a bid on phase 2 which included all the main subcontract works as provisional sums.

Ernest Ireland first became involved with the project at the 'pre-qualification' interview held at the offices of the architect. It soon became apparent that the scheme would require the design team and the contractor to work very closely together to ensure the correct placing of the main subcontracts and the successful completion of the scheme.

Having submitted a tender, Ernest Ireland were invited to interview the proposed main subcontractors. This exercise was carried out using the procedures recently developed by Ernest Ireland and British Standards under BS 5750, *Quality Assurance*,

Ernest Ireland being the first building contractor to be registered in 1988.

Ernest Ireland were awarded the contract in December 1988 and commenced work on phase 1 at the beginning of February 1989.

Phase 1

At the start of phase 1, careful planning was required to co-ordinate the excavation, sheet piling and dewatering operations.

The engineers, Ove Arup & Partners, had decided to design a raft foundation. Clearly, this was a major diverence from the piled foundations used in the area and previously designed for this project. It was a requirement of the design to keep the groundwater level 1 m below formation at all times.

The borehole soil descriptions indicated that ground conditions were at or beyond the lower effective limit of well-point dewatering, even if bentonite seals had been used. The best alternative was to design and install a vacuum pressure-ejector system. Ejectors of 50 mm dia. were introduced at 4 m centres around the perimeter of the excavation, and sand drains at 10 m grids in the main area. It was also a design requirement to maintain the 1 m drawdown below blinding level for a period of one month after the completion of the concrete raft.

The system was installed by W. J. Engineering Resources Ltd and the design checked by Mowlem Ground Engineering. Performance was monitored by piezometers strategically placed around the excavation, and pressure sensors fitted to alarms such that any faults or leaks were immediately noticed.

To Ernest Ireland, as the contractor responsible for the dewatering domestic subcontract, the programming of this work was critical. Dewatering drawdown, although a science, is somewhat unpredictable. However, forecasts proved accurate and raft construction commenced during the third week of March 1989.

The raft was designed to be 1·6 m thick, and to avoid the build-up of high temperatures during construction, 40 mm aggregate was used and 70% blast-furnace slag was substituted for ordinary Portland cement. However, in some areas spacing of the reinforcement bars was so dense that 20 mm aggregate had to be used, and the availability of concrete containing 40 mm aggregate proved difficult for the contractor to obtain.

Once the raft had been substantially completed, the upper levels of concrete deck progressed at an average cycle time of four weeks per level.

In all, 5460 m³ of concrete were used up to level 4, and 834 t of reinforcement fixed. The bolts were cast in ready to accept the first columns of the steel frame on programme during August 1989.

Phase 2

The frame design had been developed to allow the steelwork erection to be fixed and plumbed on a two-level cycle, each cycle being completed within four weeks. This enabled the permanent metal decking and concreting operation to follow closely behind the frame.

There were some 90 t of steelwork per floor, with an overall total of 600 t. The floors were formed using Holorib preformed metal decking 0·9 mm thick, with 130 mm of lightweight concrete reinforced with A142 mesh.

The levels 12 and 13 floor slabs were completed on schedule by the beginning of February 1990, about twelve months into the contract period.

The cladding and roof finishes are running towards a date of 30 May 1990 for the building to be watertight.

The curtain walling is being installed by Antlerport Ltd. An aluminium framework is designed to support part-glazed and part-panelled façades.

The glass, supplied by Luxguard of Belgium, includes double-glazed units weighing up to 259 kg each. These were installed from the floors using a specially designed gantry.

Work has commenced on the mechanical and electrical installation, particularly in the lower four levels of car park, where substantial extract ducting is required to evacuate smoke from the building in the event of a fire. The mechanical and electrical engineers are Ferguson & Partners.

Management structure

The success of the construction operation so far is due to many factors: the most important of these must be the ability and dedication of the site management team.

The project was undertaken in the knowledge that the ideal situation of all information being available at the start was clearly not possible. It was therefore essential to set up regular fortnightly information meetings, at which the contractor and design team discussed in detail the progress of the design and where resources should be directed to avoid delays.

Ernest Ireland's Contracts Manager had not only a strong construction team but also the strength of an on-site mechanical and electrical co-ordinator, a site planner with on-site computerized programming facility, and a quality assurance engineer. These individuals are able to assist the manager in his efforts to avoid areas of conflict that would in turn delay the progress of the work.

Conclusion

Although with hindsight it could have been advantageous for the contractor to have been involved at an earlier point along the design route, this does not in any way diminish the remarkable achievement of getting the project up and running on a 'fast build' programme under the JCT 80 form of contract.

RAF Support Command headquarters, Brampton

Background and early stages

J. G. CHISNALL, Director of Design, PSA Projects

On the evening of 25 October 1985, a fire at RAF Brampton, Cambridgeshire, destroyed the office accommodation for the headquarters of RAF Support Command. As it was vital for Command to continue its operations, the provision of new permanent accommodation was a priority.

What makes this project interesting is the way it was tackled both technically and contractually. Technically it was a quality engineered structure prefabricated off site. The form of contract was single-stage single-tender design and build.

The client was the Ministry of Defence (MoD) and the Royal Air Force Organisation Branch, who defined what was required and provided the finance. The government agent for the design and construction was the Property Services Agency (PSA) and its Directorate of Works for the RAF, both normally committed to the principle of a building being fully planned and designed before work can start on site.

The project objective was to replace the burnt-down building in as short a time as possible within accepted constraints of cost, space and quality. The building was to be complete within two years of receipt of the final client brief.

The Director of Defence Services at the PSA dedicated one person to lead a small team of key MoD/PSA personnel, with the responsibility of identifying the right procurement solution within the scope of the client's objective.

The following design, tender and construction constraints were identified

(*a*) time — to provide the completed building within two years
(*b*) quality — to satisfy the client and PSA in terms of quality, performance, detailing etc.
(*c*) value for money — to balance total costs of design and procurement in the context of timescales.

(The client's contract department would require strong argument to support any approach which diverged from normal tendering procedures.)

The immediate task for the team was to assess as realistically as possible the likely gross floor area and to obtain an appropriate yardstick of cost that reflected the desired quality.

The following basic design decisions were taken at an early stage. The building would be a three-storey naturally ventilated building with double courtyard. A planning grid of $4 \cdot 0$ m $\times$ $1 \cdot 2$ m would be used, which closely matched the scales of accommodation entitlement. The eventual building would be about 10 000 m^2.

The target cost of the building was defined by reference to a library of cost data operated by the PSA and the Royal Institution of Chartered Surveyors. Before the target cost was finalized, adjustments were made for extraneous items such as piled foundations and single-stage tender.

At the point where the PSA team had finalized the accommodation requirements in sketch-plan form, a direct approach was made to the local authority for approval of the basic concept, siting and scale of the building.

To achieve the project objective, certain conditions had to be accepted as fundamental.

(*a*) Total single-minded dedication and commitment would have to be given by all involved, including client, PSA and contractor.
(*b*) The normal sequence of briefing, design, tender and construction, involving full preplanning and competitive tendering, was unlikely to meet the timescale. These activities would have to be carried out in parallel.
(*c*) The early appointment of a contractor who could offer a proven fast-build method of construction, which combined

speed with traditional architectural design, would benefit the savings in design and construction time required.

(d) Client approvals would have to be swiftly given.

(e) No changes could be made beyond final sketch plans or approved contractor's design.

(f) No design changes could be made during the construction stage.

The PSA investigated a number of contractors which were able to offer a method of building to achieve the earliest possible construction and also meet the requirements in terms of flexibility in design, quality and time. Conder's 'dry envelope' method of construction offered a unique solution in that its flexibility allowed for variety in architectural design within a few acceptable constraints. The principal benefits of the dry envelope were

(a) maximization of prefabrication in controlled factory conditions

(b) comprehensive library of pre-designed details

(c) tried and tested on over 1000 projects

(d) rapid site assembly reducing construction time by creating a weathertight enclosure at a very early stage

(e) certainty of completion on time.

The PSA team's examination of the different contractual options and their comparative programmes demonstrated that a fully preplanned project exceeded the time-scale considerably (Table 1). The team resolved that the best way forward was a single-tender

Table 1. *Alternative approaches*

	Times for design and construction	Relative cost of design, resource and construction: %
Traditional fully preplanned	3 years 3 months	100
Accelerated traditional	2 years 10 months	101
Two-stage develop and construct	2 years 9 months	104
Single-stage, single-tender design and build	1 year 9 months	108

approach with Conder, provided that they satisfied themselves that this would meet the time constraints, and that an acceptable cost could be agreed.

In summary, the single-tender approach was as follows.

(*a*) The market was researched.
(*b*) PSA experience with Conder was researched.
(*c*) A cost target was set by PSA and the client.
(*d*) Preliminary discussions were held with Conder to validate the cost target.
(*e*) A cost plan was agreed with Conder.
(*f*) The cost of Conder elements (dry envelope) was identified and agreed.

Management decisions made by the client and PSA at feasibility stage undoubtedly led to successful design and construction techniques being adopted, and excellent team spirit between client and contractor throughout the design and construction stages.

Design and construction

A. K. PENSON, Managing Director, Conder Projects, and J. E. WEST, Group Marketing Director, Conder Group plc

Winning the contract
At the time of Conder's initial appointment, the PSA team's objective was to get work started on site. This involved completing several tasks rapidly.

(*a*) A Conder Project Manager was appointed to the project and he was dedicated to act as the single point of responsibility with the client and to lead and manage the design and construction team.
(*b*) The design team was selected and appointed after careful vetting of suitable professional practices which were accustomed to dry-envelope construction and to designing within the constraints of a 'fast-build' programme.

25

(c) Conder's design and construct technique had to be introduced to the client. This involved making several presentations to the RAF Support Command.

(d) There had to be a series of meetings to define the programme, resolve remaining design details and, above all, initiate the managerial structure which would ensure an effective transfer of responsibility for design to Conder.

(e) The PSA team had to produce a final sketch plan and a performance brief describing the standard of materials and workmanship which would form the basis of the contract documents on which an offer could be submitted.

Between March and May 1986, continuous dialogue was maintained between Conder and the PSA on all matters relating to space planning, internal design, elevations, specification and choice and quality of materials. This resulted in the original concept drawings prepared by the PSA being adopted, avoiding the need for future consultation and reappraisal by the RAF.

While the final design was under consideration by the PSA, Conder was able to prepare a final tender and programme planned to meet the target completion date set by the PSA. Once Conder had offered the PSA an acceptable total package then, as the project proceeded, all quotations for the work would be available for examination. At pre-order stage Conder interviewed every sub-contractor and insisted that each one supplied its own site management to ensure a high standard of quality control. Conder offered a price and time to build that it would guarantee, and operated an open-book tendering procedure. This design and tender programme was completed in seven weeks from initial briefing to final tender.

The excellent rapport between Conder and the PSA convinced the Agency that it could step back from the direct executive control. The overall approach convinced the PSA's Contracts Division that the contract would meet the criteria of public accountability. The scene was set for the onward design development and construction, with a remaining programme of just 18 months.

The instruction to Conder to commence detailed design was received on 30 May 1986; construction was to start on 23 June 1986.

Planning and contract management

Overall project planning was the key issue in maintaining the momentum of the tight design and construction programme. This was achieved by the preparation of a critical path design-and-subcontract packages procurement programme incorporating approvals, materials and manufacturing lead times.

Regular liaison was maintained with the client to ensure that client approval for design and subcontract tenders was obtained in sufficient time for the construction programme to be maintained on site.

Control was maintained by

(*a*) close control of subcontractors' performance
(*b*) weekly progress meetings between Conder and subcontractors' resident site management
(*c*) fortnightly meetings between the Project Manager and the contract management of subcontractors with their respective teams, attended when necessary by the design consultants to provide for immediate design query information requirements
(*d*) regular meetings of the design development team, held at least every four weeks, and held prior to client review meetings to identify matters for immediate client clarification or approval
(*e*) client progress meetings which followed the meetings of the Project Design Team, the client team joining the project team, including professional consultants, to review all aspects of the project
(*f*) regular review of quality, safety and cost goals.

Conder's approach to the construction challenge was governed by strict site circumstances.

(*a*) The roads to and within the site had to be kept open and clear at all times.
(*b*) There were the restrictions of working within a high-security establishment.
(*c*) All construction work (e.g. auger piling) had to be carried out with the minimum of disturbance to RAF personnel.

(The site was auger-piled, with some 600 piles, 13 m deep. This was due partly to the suitability of the clay soil, with a very high water table, and partly to the proximity of surrounding buildings and services, particularly a delicate fibre-optic communications cable.)

The sequence of operations for grubbing up the old foundations, piles, pile caps and ground beams and replacement with new, was phased to the fast dry-envelope erection programme, which was totally complete by January 1987, and internal trades progressed uninterrupted by the winter weather.

Quality assurance was a key factor and the PSA expected a guarantee that its criteria for quality as well as cost and speed of construction would be met. Conder was able to give these assurances and has subsequently become the first company to be awarded QA registration for superstructure and cladding.

Urgent design changes to the calorifiers were established as necessary, along with the re-manufacture and testing of equipment, because it transpired that the temperature of the incoming steam main was lower than specified by the client brief. The concern was that this would have serious effect on the completion of the installation and its final commissioning. To reduce the delay to the contract, meetings were held with the PSA and relevant subcontractors to discuss the options. The result was that Conder completed two of the three floors ready for fitting out by the RAF to its original critical programme.

Within the programme, Conder was able to accommodate £600 000 worth of additional RAF requirements

(a) a building management system and a Lamson tube (a compressed-air delivery system) linked to the base control at the main entrance
(b) a flood relief scheme to remove a long-standing problem
(c) secure computer rooms and part replacement of the existing electrical main.

Conder was also required to undertake fitting out, normally arranged directly by the PSA.

Conclusion

The spirit of co-operation and team spirit throughout on the part of the client, PSA, Conder, the design team and the subcontractors proved a positive factor in the success of the project, something which was identified as paramount to the success of the project from the outset.

Brampton was completed, on time, on 24 December 1987, and fitting out followed to allow the client's occupation on 5 March 1988.

Broadgate, London: phases 5, 9 and 10

A client's perspective

P. W. ROGERS, Construction Director, Stanhope Properties plc

Stanhope Properties' strategy is 'to produce developments which create a sense of place, combining aesthetic appeal and architectural merit with efficiency in construction and use, and which command premium rents in locations with excellent growth prospects'.

Fast build must be put into the context of fast project implementation: taking the project from conception to the earliest possible use by tenants. Stanhope's objective is to produce buildings faster and more economically than industry standards (by reducing out-turn construction costs and funding charges in particular). To achieve this objective requires attention to research, efficient design, and efficient management.

Research

Who are Stanhope's customers? They are all of those involved in the development process, from the investor through local authorities to the occupier. Research identifies who the customers are and their wants and needs into the future. On Broadgate, detailed research identified the occupiers' requirements for modern, well serviced, high-quality office space, capable of accommodating high levels of information technology and space for open-floor trading.

On large mixed development projects, the aspirations of the local community and their needs for amenities, housing, recreation, training and other facilities are researched and brought into the master planning. The results of such work ensure that the local communities' wants are satisfied and that the project sensitively creates a sense of place within the local environment.

Research into specific user needs led to Stanhope pioneering the shell and core concept in the UK. Occupiers are now able to finish buildings to suit their own specific requirements, without wasting time and money on unwanted finishes. Use of this technique also permits even earlier access by the tenant using phased hand-overs and occupation.

Detailed research minimizes the inherent speculative risks of the property development process and secures tenants at the earliest opportunity. Reduction of these risks facilitates the funding process, making schemes more attractive to joint venture partners and financiers. Research is carried out by external consultants and embraces value analysis, space planning, market analysis, financial sources and economic trends.

Environmental issues are continually assessed to ensure the maximum efficiency of the company's buildings while maintaining a sensitivity to the depletion of world resources.

The selection of materials which brings value to the company's products while contributing to ease of fabrication or construction is essential. Methods are assessed which by standardization of components simplify the on-site activities. The fabrication of complex items off site, where they can be more effectively controlled, and minimizing the complexity of site logistics encourages modularization such as the implementation of toilet-pods.

Management techniques used in North America, Japan and Europe have also been analysed in depth, and, where appropriate, adapted.

By continued evaluation and feedback, the company is able to ensure that future products respond to the changing needs of the business and the community, and that its design and construction techniques are continually assessed.

Stanhope's research has led it to understand better the needs of its customers, and that these vary considerably. No doubt for the future the demographic changes will influence the working environment that will be expected by all employees. Much of the current stock of offices is out of date and inappropriate for an organization based on information technology (IT), and unacceptable from the end-user's point of view.

Clearly, customer overspecification of requirements has traditionally led to increased costs without enhancing the value. An example is a customer's estimation of its electrical power requirements, where measurement by Stanhope after occupation has shown installed capacity has been over twice actual customer usage.

The building industry in the UK is an anachronism relying on traditional methods which it can no longer sustain, and which too often sacrifices quality and value in its efforts to reduce costs. Similarly, its methods are based on conflict and complex structures which are counteractive to fast communication, positive attitudes and an innovative approach.

Efficient design

Stanhope's success demonstrates that quality architecture 'sells' buildings, by achieving efficient construction and use of materials, and higher rents. Hence, one of the hallmarks of Stanhope developments is the quality of the design teams. To facilitate the design process, Stanhope has developed a brief which sets the minimum design standards, is responsive to ideas and to items identified by research, and is sensitive to the environment. Minimum standards having been set, the architect and designers are given the maximum freedom in which to develop the design.

The Stanhope philosophy requires and relies on a 'hands-on' approach during the design development. By regular internal review, the company's considerable in-house development, design and construction expertise ensures that buildings are created matching the specific objectives and maintaining a sense of corporate identity and image.

Flexibility for future tenants' needs is also considered during the design process (for example, the ability to adapt space by flooring over or opening up atria; provision of 'soft spots' for expansion of IT or other tenant-specific services). Similarly, the concept of shell and core enables the occupiers to finish their buildings to suit their own specific requirements.

The construction manager is an integral part of the professional team. By being in direct contact with the designers, he can ensure that the design proposals reflect workable and buildable solutions right from the outset of design.

By detailed value analysis, the company can ensure that product quality is further enhanced without a commensurate increase in price or loss in quality.

The organizational structure with construction management places the client in direct contact with trade contractors. This arrangement ensures that the architect, designers and construction manager can do what they are best at without being fettered within contractual frameworks, and without distancing the technical inputs from the trade contractor away from the design team. Close contact between the trade contractor and the design team ensures rapid approval and checking and also enables the trade contractor to be part of the design process without going through an intermediary. This promotes the opportunity for real design alternatives and ensures that buildability is effectively considered.

Efficient management

The Stanhope strategy is to use construction management for all projects. Stanhope appoints an in-house Project Manager, who is accountable for all aspects of the project and has the authority to act on the company's behalf. Having a single operating point ensures a clear management structure, thus facilitating rapid decision-making and focusing communication. Pre-construction and construction activities are closely and pro-actively managed by the construction manager.

Before construction is started, the design and planning must be substantially complete; and 70% by value of all the design and work-package documentation must be bid before the job commences. Stanhope projects are fast build but not fast track! This control ensures that the company has a very good fix on the end-value construction cost before any commitments are made. This minimizes the risks associated with fast track.

To be able to achieve short but realistic construction periods requires meticulous research into the availability of resources (materials, components and contractors). This is successfully achieved not only by the development and maintenance of data banks but also by creation of the right environment for the project teams to trade and exchange ideas and information.

Part of Stanhope's construction strategy is to manufacture as many elements of the project as is possible off site. In the off-site environment, quality is better managed and costs controlled. Use of this technique can also substantially shorten the critical paths. It is important to be continually on the look-out for innovative techniques which speed up the construction process; this in turn requires the open team input to allow exchanges of ideas.

The success of fast build relies on effective quality management and a 'right first time' attitude. Quality cannot be effectively controlled by an oppressive (and manpower-consuming) paperwork bureaucracy. Reliance on the individual to perform to high quality standards is achieved by management instilling the right culture and motivating by providing the right environment. Stanhope defines quality through customers' needs and perceptions, through the construction manager, through research and through feedback from its customers.

The company has developed its own terms of appointment and contracts for use with the design team, construction manager and trade contractors. All parties are contracted on an equal footing with single point responsibility clearly established. The contracts are lump sum, fixed price and fixed duration and include no bills of quantities or other expenses, allowing the contractors to manage the contract for profit rather than the work.

Stanhope's contracts clearly identify each party's obligations, are fair, provide incentives to trade contractors (for example, by quick direct payment for work completed) and promote the formation of long term relationships based on mutual trust. The company sees itself as a hard but fair employer.

Trade contractors are able to perform with the maximum freedom against performance specifications and are able to plan their own methodology, both in the global and work-front senses. They are responsible for co-ordinating their activities with those contractors that interface with them. Early involvement with the trade contractor during the design process ensures the production of efficient designs, and ensures that the interfaces are identified and properly managed.

The Stanhope way requires all members of the team to take a new approach and have a positive 'can do' attitude. The use of construction management facilitates rapid and easy communication and dialogue between members of the team. To ensure that everybody understands Stanhope's philosophy, the company undertakes a series of induction courses, starting with the architect right through to the shop floor.

Stanhope is committed to industrial training and the welfare and safety of all operatives. It is important that operators perform to their best ability and that a sense of pride is instilled into all levels of the project team. Stanhope believes in identifying good performance and does, by regular review, give out awards (and brickbats) to deserving companies and individuals. The company's project managers ensure that the whole team is motivated and that people work in a good environment where relationships at all levels are well respected.

Conclusion

Stanhope's success is based on the intelligent use of research and the better understanding of its customers' requirements. The company has demonstrated that carefully planned design to the highest standards of quality provides a better product quicker. Stanhope places great importance on effective management, which together with a positive attitude provides better control. Building faster has been achieved by research, efficient design, and efficient management. Clearly, user research combined with carefully managed design produces a better investment, faster and at a better price.

A construction manager's point of view

I. G. MACPHERSON, Bovis—Schal Joint Venture, now Managing Director, Mace Ltd

Broadgate established new production standards for the industry. For the first time the tables were turned in comparisons between

Table 1. *Performance comparisons*

	Floor area constructed: m^2/week	
	USA	UK
USA/UK study, 1978: average	269	158
USA/UK study, 1986: average	216	169
Fastest known US building	473	
Fastest known UK building: Broadgate		
Phase 1		247
Phase 2		574
Phase 3		627

the UK and the USA. Table 1 shows the results of studies by Reading University carried out in 1978, 1986 and 1988.

These new standards of rate of build were not established easily. The paper describes some of the factors which I believe were major contributors to this result.

The paper refers to phase 5 and phases 9 and 10. Outline project descriptions are given in Table 2, and key statistics in Table 3.

Construction management

The management system chosen by Rosehaugh Stanhope was construction management. Stanhope champions this form of contract across the wide range of projects it executes, and the principals of that company were the pioneers of construction management in the UK.

The construction manager is appointed as the client's professional to manage the construction team from the earliest design stage through to practical completion. In this he orchestrates the process by active involvement in each area of it. He is not there to interfere but to encourage and direct co-operation between designer and client, designer and trade contractor, and so on. He is in effect an extension of the client's organization. He is paid a fee for this service and this is his only source of profit from the project. Because of the construction manager's closeness to the client, and the professional orientation of fee arrangements, the construction manager's objectives are exactly the same as the client's.

Table 2. *Outline project descriptions*

	Phase 5	Phases 9 and 10
Floor area	340 000 ft² gross	480 000 ft² gross
Number of storeys	8	8
Frame type	Steel; 25 weeks	Concrete; 25 weeks
Cladding type	Strongback curtain wall: aluminium, glass and granite (UK)	Precast concrete (Belgium)

Table 3. *Key statistics*

Steel	2230 tons; 25 weeks
Concrete	1100 m² in one pour; peak output 4300 m² in one week
Formwork strip time	36–48 hours
Curtain wall, phase 5	8790 m²; 6 months
Curtain wall, phases 9 and 10	12 500 m²; 6 months

Construction management is a client-orientated service and needs to be independent of the normal structural relationships in place in the industry.

Construction management is an *attitude* first and foremost. The construction manager must always be hyperactive in pushing the teams not only to achieve targets but to beat them. To achieve this the construction manager's staff need to be highly skilled — not only in the technical knowledge they hold, but also in the area of human relations. Only by skill in the latter can the shift in attitudes be achieved. It is difficult for other professionals in the team to suddenly accept fundamental questioning from someone not actually in the client's organization. It is also difficult for trade contractors to be persuaded to drop their old defence mechanisms or to be open and honest in their criticism of design and management. ('That guy might be sitting on the next job selection panel'.) This is an area where the construction manager can generate major improvements in the future. But these attitudes need to be and are being changed by sensitive managers, showing that these very processes improve the ability of all members of the team to satisfy their own and the client's objectives.

Construction management should generate an environment where people profit from their efforts, not lose money. This was achieved in the main on phase 5 and phases 9 and 10, but with some pain.

As part of this process the construction manager must generate with the client an open environment where problems are solved without fear of recrimination. A problem found by a team member is a problem adopted, not one to be passed on as quickly as possible to some unsuspecting fall guy! Contractual relationships are guides, not barriers.

Only by the construction manager's staff being 'hands on' from the Managing Director through the whole team can this kind of encouragement and support be given. Remote management is too easy, and those who enjoy their golf handicap should stay out of construction management. Broadgate was a partnership: participation and gain-sharing with all the people connected with the project therefore was endemic.

In construction management the client places all trade contractors direct, and therefore a special bond is created as well as a far more efficient and beneficial financial arrangement being generated. All trade contractors are placed on a lump-sum fixed-price basis. Before a package is bought, the designer must complete his element design 100%. Before work starts in the field, 70% by value should be tested in the market.

Construction management is about fast build, not fast track, although, as shown earlier, it still results in overall design and construction times being shorter.

Skills such as cost planning and value analysis are central to construction management as well. These skills must not be departmentalized but must be part of the training of the construction manager's Project Manager. It should not be necessary for the construction manager to have a surveyor sitting at his knee to talk cost!

Value analysis (or value engineering) is a proven management tool which uses logical and creative techniques to seek out the best functional balance between cost, reliability and performance of a product or project. Wherever possible cost is reduced, but without detriment to either performance or quality. Only by the independence of mind generated by the change of attitude in construction management can value engineering be properly exercised in an unfettered way.

Both cost planning and value engineering are new and, particularly in the former, construction managers have much work to do to establish high levels of proficiency, which hitherto have been seen as the quantity surveyor's domain. It is also important to involve everyone in the team in value engineering: it must not be an isolated event.

The construction manager must constantly be questioning and providing ideas for review, and innovation in thinking should at all times be encouraged. Ideas are the fuel of good management.

In all of this, the people in the team must not only feel that they have achieved something worthwhile but that that effort and achievement have been rewarded, and a regular client-led programme of rewards is part of this.

Key management features

What, then, were the key management features which made Broadgate work as a construction management project?

First, Bovis—Schal were appointed virtually on 'day 1', when design had barely started, and 'set' ideas had not taken root. Through this the construction manager understood more the reasons for design decisions and strategies and could respond to them more intelligently, and with knowledge of the designer's aims as well as the client's objectives. Design and construction strategies could be developed together, without time-wasting re-design.

Bovis—Schal prepared the market for this project by early discussion, well in advance of bidding, to give trade contractors early notice of the project, and to give them opportunities to discuss what the project was aiming to achieve. Through this period Bovis—Schal were able to build up relationships with people, not just companies, and to encourage them to participate in the development of construction strategies, methods and programming. Also value engineering took place, with the trade contractors fully participating, by focusing the team with its expertise in developing specifications and design. This process also ensures that when bids go out they are in a condition of stability from a cost, time and quality stance. During this process the team can clearly define the 'scope' of work in each package so that trade contractors are not being asked to carry out work which is alien or disruptive to their organizations.

Buying of the packages must be by line management, not the traditionally used buying departments. Indeed, good construction management must be operated by the managers in the project teams, and never by people outside it. It is important that through this process the manager responsible for buying is 'hands-on' in the production process as well. This gives continuity to involvement, ensuring that there are no breaks in understanding of what has been bought, as well as ensuring a continuing bond between managers in the construction management and trade contractor teams.

Cost planning and value engineering go hand in hand, and are intrinsically linked to buying as well. The construction manager develops the cost plan in a way that reflects how the project is to be constructed. Elemental breakdown and how the project is to be bought must be key elements in this. The cost plan should be a real working document, fully understood by the team and structured in such a way as to be used as a cost control document by everyone. It should be user-friendly.

Value engineering has its maximum value early in the project: the impact lessens as the project timetable develops.

For Bovis—Schal value engineering is the process whereby the construction manager challenges or confirms the building economics. It goes beyond buildability.

At Broadgate Bovis—Schal gave positive advice on maximization of site usage and enhancing value where it was most beneficial to the client. That meant, for instance, on concentrating funds in the visual areas such as lobbies where prospective tenants are most influenced.

The process flows over the whole construction approach. Should the frame be built in steel or concrete taking account of all the conditions that would affect cost, not just the straight design/cost comparison? How can the building be clad to achieve the visual requirements of the architect? Strong back or concrete: what is the most cost-effective solution in the market place that respects the parameters?

To make value engineering truly effective the construction manager must be respected by the architect who, in turn, must be receptive to positive proposals. Value engineering is not just cutting costs at the expense of architecture. It is enhancing value and using money where it will be most effective.

Further advantage of early involvement of trade contractors is that they contribute in a positive way to developing the construction strategy. Logistics can be decided, materials management disciplines agreed. At Broadgate, hoists were specially designed and built so that manhandling of materials was kept to an absolute minimum. For example, plasterboard could be offloaded from trailers on pallets on to wheeled trolleys which fitted into hoists, then wheeled off at appropriate floor levels to the place of work. Plasterboard was delivered shrink-wrapped and was not touched by human hand until it was put into place on a wall. The project's hoists were the only ones in the UK which could cope with this level of materials management. This was a function of 'listening' to the trade contractors and doing something about the stupidities which are entrenched in this industry. It was also a result of not being restrained by the off-line members of the building team, more concerned with various budgetary elements than the broader productivity and cost efficiency of this project.

Controlling the project should also be a hands-on process, not a bureaucratic or paper-laden effort. The company introduced meetings on a two-weekly basis for the directors of the trade contractors involved to meet with the client's Project Director and the construction manager's Project Director, with designers in attendance. These were short and sharp meetings to deal only with the key issues delaying the project. The Joint Venture used them to reward publicly good effort, achievement and quality.

As well as this, the Joint Venture introduced trade supervisors' meetings two or three times a week at 7.30 a.m. to deal with the more detailed day to day problems which needed to be resolved.

Both these meetings ensured hands-on involvement from directors to supervisors: it also, and most importantly, encouraged problem-solving between trade contractors at every level.

A further positive and continuing factor was that the Joint Venture held induction courses for all those who came to join the project as members of the management team. There was a full day of sessions attended by the client, the designer, the construction manager and the trade contractors. All participants were asked to contribute, and there they started the process of thinking about the whole project, not just an isolated element.

Project co-ordination took many forms. Mechanical and electrical co-ordination was dealt with by a series of 'hostage' meetings, where the group of trade contractors involved in services and interfacing trades would meet over an eight-week period and discuss their elements, and then a common negative would circulate, with each succeeding trade adding its element as discussed. At the end of this period the project had been co-ordinated, and only minor co-ordination problems accrued after this. The meetings generated 'team spirit' and a common objective, which was to everyone's advantage. People were committed. Those things which threw a spanner in the works were late changes, which really did have a very bad chain reaction. In the future, changes should be dealt with as a separate retrofit.

Designers' attitudes are obviously important as well, and an illustration of an openness of mind and spirit was the structural frame for phases 9 and 10. The designers, Skidmore, Owings & Merrill, developed a design, which Bovis—Schal then took to the trade contractor market; one company came back with a totally different solution, which it could argue was more efficient and time-responsive. Skidmore, Owings & Merrill concurred and changed their design. Not many UK design practices would be as open and responsive as this. This decision saved the client his money, and achieved a high-quality product at the end.

Construction management is in the mould of 'can do' (not 'ah, there's a problem'). Broadgate was epitomized by this attitude, and only those who were unable to accept it totally failed.

The key factors of success are summarized in Table 4. Behind these are the basic principles listed in Table 5, which underline the construction management approach at Broadgate.

Table 4.   Key factors of success

Induction courses for management
Buying process
Open forum and design development
Hands-on approach
Incentives and rewards
Direct relationships between client and trade contractors
Can-do attitudes
Value engineering process
Construction manager's position in the team as an equal professional
Client involvement
Designer's attitudes to construction management skills

Future improvements

What can be improved next time? Design management pre- and post-buy needs to be sharper and much more tightly controlled. The construction manager must take responsibility for this fully, and the client should recognize this responsibility and discipline himself for it as well, within the framework set out by the construction manager. Designs need to be more acutely attuned

Table 5.   Basic principles of construction management

Success and rewards (prompt payment, fair treatment financially)
Non-confrontational attitudes
Teamwork
Relationships and trust
'Design before you start' (this was not always achieved, which resulted in cost and time overruns)
Clear understanding of roles and risks
Equitable contracts
Clear responsibilities
People-'care': management of safety, health and welfare, and industrial relations
Standardization of components
Build in the factory, not on site
Attitude: can-do
A problem found is a problem adopted (a problem-solving environment)
No 'them' and 'us'
Openness in management style (e.g. meetings of trade contractor directors)
Relative importance of time, cost and quality
Training and induction courses
Access to management: open-door policy
Claims mentality-v-getting on with the job — resources where they should be
Bettering the industry (a real factor); people-satisfaction (pride in the project)
Relationships between client and trade contractor, and construction manager and designer
Hands-on management
Short lines of communication
Ability to contribute technical innovation
Trade-to-trade management and supervision
Promoting trade contractor stand alone capacity

to a 'design change regime': no design changes after buy, and no design 'development' smudging post-buy.

More value engineering effort is required to improve the overall result of design and construction, especially in the early stages.

The selection of trade contractors needs to be more rigorous in terms of off-site resources and staff capability.

Off-site monitoring needs to be more effective, with simple systems which are user-friendly.

Induction should be developed to include operatives as well. A greater understanding leads to better attitudes.

Materials management disciplines on and off site need to be clearly understood and managed by all. The construction manager needs to properly set up and disicpline the systems.

The level of off-site production of components should be increased in order to add value to the project and provide more security overall.

Paperwork could be cut down by simplifying and managing the project systems — not just using them as a device to buy time or change minds!

The construction manager's staff should be of higher calibre and there should be fewer of them. Stand-alone managers with a rounded ability are needed.

Conclusion

Only in the client-led construction-management environment can the right attitudes become inherent in the teams: only by the breakdown of the old hierarchical management and control structures can the energies released by real construction management be realized, to the client's benefit.

CARE: customers are really everything.

A designer's point of view

T. K. FRIDSTEIN, Director, Skidmore, Owings & Merrill Inc.

The Broadgate complex in the City of London, developed by
Rosehaugh Stanhope Developments, is built over and around
British Rail Liverpool Street Station. The development comprises
14 office buildings, two major urban squares, shopping and
amenities, totalling over 6×10^6 ft^2. The first four buildings were
designed by Arup Associates and completed in 1988. The
remaining ten buildings were designed by Skidmore, Owings &
Merrill, beginning in 1986, with construction to be completed in
1991. The entire complex has been built through construction
management, with Bovis the construction manager for the first
group of buildings and Bovis—Schal the construction manager for
the others. The two buildings discussed here, phase 5 and phases
9 and 10, are representative of the complex and between them
demonstrate a wide range of design and construction issues.

Phase 5, now owned and occupied by Bankers Trust and known
as 1 Appold Street, was the second office building completed of
the Skidmore, Owings & Merrill phases. It comprises 340 000 ft^2
of office accommodation, a major leisure centre and a pub. It is
a steel-frame building with typical clear span of 18 m. The building
has eight floors, with typical floor-to-floor height of 4.23 m,
allowing for 2.74 m clear above a 200 mm raised floor. The
cladding is a panellized granite and glass system. The building
is fully air-conditioned, with fan rooms located on each floor, and
a central chilled-water plant. Construction began in April 1987
and practical completion was achieved in October 1988.

Phases 9 and 10 comprise Broadwalk House, located at the
corner of Appold Street and Primrose Street. The building is
occupied by Ashurst Morris and Crisp and Alexander Laing
Cruikshank Holdings. It has 480 000 ft^2 of offices and rises eight
storeys. Parking for 175 cars is located on two levels below grade.
It has a concrete structure consisting of precast girders and in situ
slabs. The cladding is pigmented precast concrete designed to
resemble terracotta. The mechanical systems are similar to those
of phase 5, with floor-by-floor fan rooms and a central chilled-

water and boiler plant serving a variable-air-volume distribution system and perimeter radiation. The toilets, as for all Broadgate buildings, are entirely prefabricated off site. Design began in February 1987. Construction started in December 1987 and practical completion was achieved in April 1989. Broadwalk House was completed within the projected programme and for less than the estimated cost plan.

These buildings were produced with a construction management approach. It is unlikely that this level of quality, cost control and speed could have been achieved under another form of contracting.

Effectiveness of construction management

Construction management was instrumental in this process, first, because it promotes a team approach during design and construction. Vital preconstruction advice is given to the designers by the person responsible for the final construction. Most of the decisions that affect the quality, cost and constructability of a building are made during the concept design stages. Once the drawings are completed, it is too late to make fundamental changes without totally disrupting the project programme and costs. With the construction manager actually a part of the design effort, the most effective designs can be achieved.

Further, being involved in the initial design process, the construction manager has a better understanding of the project: why decisions are made and what this impact may be. This allows the construction manager to better plan and construct the building.

Second, construction management allows for elemental design and procurement. Each element of the building can be studied, designed and tendered for individually as required. Some elements require more analysis and review than others. Some must be procured in advance of others. The construction management process permits appropriate attention to be given to individual elements without negatively impacting the design programme. Each major element will follow a design programme as follows.

(a) *Concept design alternatives.* Alternative concepts will be proposed by the designer, with input and review by the owner and construction manager.

(b) *Pricing/constructability analysis.* The construction manager will advise on the pricing and construction implications of the various concepts.

(*c*) *Trade contractor review.* Selected trade contractors may be consulted. These are the people who best understand their particular expertise and they can help maximize the effectiveness and practicality of a design.

(*d*) *Final design.* The result of all the analysis, review and consultation is incorporated into the final design documents.

(*e*) *Procurement.* The client, the designer and the construction manager together agree the list of tenderers. The results of the tender are openly reviewed by this team and a collective decision is made regarding the award of each trade contract.

The benefits of this process are best demonstrated by examples. Broadwalk House has a concrete structure because the construction manager advised that, while a steel structure would cost the same, a concrete structure required less lead-in time and would save three months of construction. This input, delivered early during concept design, was based on discussion with the trade contractors who later tendered for the project. The cladding is also a result of intensive team interaction during the early design stages. The design intent was to use traditional terracotta technology. The construction manager evaluated the terracotta industry and reported that there was not enough capacity in the entire industry to clad this building. A precast concrete solution was then investigated. The final design was achieved through extensive discussion, with samples and drawings from trade contractors. All this could take place independently of the design and procurement of the foundation and structural systems.

Conclusion

Construction management has been essential to the success of these buildings. This team approach increases understanding, decreases adversarial tensions, and promotes an environment most conducive to solving problems such as always arise in a major project. Construction management allows the maximum information to be available to the client and designer during the critical formative stages of a project. It gives the designer the best opportunity to achieve the most effective design. Without doubt, construction management permitted these buildings to be designed and constructed in the shortest time possible. Finally, and most important, the best product was achieved because construction management allows each participant in the process, the designer, the trade contractor and the construction manager, to do what they know and do best.

A concrete trade contractor's perspective

R. G. O'ROURKE, Managing Director, R. O'Rourke & Sons Ltd

Buildability is the foundation stone of O'Rourke & Sons' philosophy and from the very beginning in 1977 the company has shown its interest in contributing to a project's structural design.

Success with precast units soon led the company to composite construction and the use of precast soffit units and simplified systems of falsework support. The company gained a foothold in the concrete frame market and it was always willing to provide an input to the overall design. This was to be its introduction to many of the leading practices in London and the South East.

The company saw the value of having its own team, and of no longer being dependent on a main contractor's site services, which could vary in quality. Above all, it saw a value to the project in its being allowed to take responsibility for all aspects of its work. With qualified people and an interface with consultants, it went ahead to develop its business and to market the concept of a stand-alone concrete frame package.

By that time management contracting was emerging as a potential market leader and the company naturally turned its attention to it. Again, there were barriers which took time and effort to overcome. Legal conditions severely limited the scope for involvement. The problem was bonding.

The client's requirement for security had led management contractors to call on other national contractors to undertake the frequently substantial substructure and superstructure packages. As an independent, the company found itself only able to bid for part of the work, and distanced even further from a management contractor's co-ordinating and reporting functions.

The breakthrough came at Hammersmith Hospital, where no bonding was required. O'Rourke won the bid to erect the phase I superstructure for Laing Management Contracting and, with their co-operation, persuaded the consulting engineers, Ove Arup & Partners, to change the design from fully in situ concrete to semi-precast. The programme was cut by twelve weeks and access was given to following trades much earlier than would otherwise have been possible.

It was then 1986, Broadgate had been started and the company was approached regarding a frame for the AMA Building. This was the first concrete-framed building to be constructed at Broadgate. Early completion was vital as it was to house relocated BR personnel, thereby releasing the construction site for phases 6 and 7. A decision had been made to build this in concrete, as the developer could not afford the lead time required for structural steel. The company tendered for, and secured, the frame package, its first experience of a construction management contract.

With Broadgate phases 9 and 10 at an outline design stage, the company was asked by Bovis—Schal to contribute ideas on programme and budgets should the client wish to construct the frame in concrete.

Broadgate: phases 9 and 10

The brief was that the project would be designed as an in situ concrete frame. The client and professional team indicated that they required a programme that would provide the frame in a period of 20−22 weeks (the theoretical period for constructing a similar frame in structural steelwork).

Preliminary drawings gave the company cause to doubt the viability of the programme, and it required an opportunity to meet with the designers. This was its introduction to the open door environment of construction management.

The company was confident that it could reduce both the overall programme and its own risks by rationalizing the sizes of principal members and introducing an element of composite construction.

First, however, it had to use all its engineering skills to convince the design team.

As part of the construction team in Broadgate's earlier phases, the company had been witness to the client's and the professional team's positive handling of day to day problems. It therefore had no reason to believe that it would not receive full co-operation in all matters of logistics and the flow of information. On account of this, and its confidence in being able to perform, the company chose to disregard such items as damages and contractual conditions when making its final assessment.

Being in competition, the company naturally required an assurance from the client and his project team that there would be no leak of its proposals. This was observed to the letter and soon became an accepted part of the open bargaining which benefits construction management.

The company agreed a base set of information upon which to bid, qualified the information and tendered a lump sum fixed price linked to a programme period. Major revisions were to be a matter of add/omit based on a schedule of unit rates submitted at the same time.

This form of contract held many attractions: the company would be able to influence the design, work with leading engineers and, above all, demonstrate to the industry that a concrete solution can be cheaper and quicker than structural steelwork.

The advantage to a project of the trade contractor's early involvement cannot be overstressed. Had the company been involved earlier, it could have cut the time taken in arriving at a final solution, and given positive assistance to the design team in the planning of materials handling and cranage.

The company's proposals undoubtedly increased productivity on the project as a whole. Not only was the programme reduced by almost three months, but individual outputs soared, resulting in 4300 m² being cast in the best week. This was a tribute to co-operation at all levels and a marker for fast build techniques in concrete construction.

Management systems

It is now the company's firm belief that contractual relationships benefit significantly from a construction management label.

The advantages of this are as follows.

As the client's agent, the construction manager does not have a vested interest in using the contract to beat the trade contractor into submission. The health of the project as a whole takes precedence.

The client is afforded a day to day knowledge of his site.

The co-ordination of trade contractors both with the project team and with each other is a reality. This discipline is further reinforced by the presence of representatives from each trade contractor at the fortnightly 'directors' meetings', as well as senior executives from the design team, the client and his construction manager. The informality of these occasions promotes a spirit of 'hands-on management' which extends to each organization.

The trade contractor *is* part of the construction team. With access to the client and the design team, he is definitely not a sub-contractor. Construction management *per se* is flat: it is not a hierarchy. This has enabled O'Rourke to develop a much deeper understanding of a client's needs and the benefits which might be gained by seeing that they are continually met.

Fast build

Fast-build techniques have given a much needed boost to innovation in concrete construction and have received both widespread publicity and stringent testing. The company believes that the value of their adoption is proven and shorter construction periods are here to stay.

The past three years have shown that O'Rourke's project teams fully appreciate the meaning of 'can do'. They know what achievement is and will be seeking to improve outputs and quality still further in the future. However, much must depend on its continuing to be involved at the earliest reasonable stage. It always will.

A steelwork trade contractor's view

R. S. MILLER, Managing Director, Octavius Atkinson & Sons Ltd

Octavius Atkinson & Sons were appointed as the steelwork trade contractor for phase 5 at Broadgate in May 1987.

The contract was for the supply, delivery and erection of 2230 t of structural steelwork and staircases. Included within the scope of the contract were the supply and installation of 30 000 m² of metal decking and the through-deck welding of 37 000 shear studs.

The company was responsible for the preparation of the fabrication detail drawings from information issued by the architect/ structural engineer, Skidmore, Owings & Merrill. That responsibility included the design of the structural connections in accordance with BS 5950.

The stability of the structure was largely achieved by the rigid-moment connections of the perimeter beams to the columns, with the concrete floors acting as horizontal diaphragms. This necessitated temporary bracing being introduced at alternate floor levels during the construction period, leading up to the placing of the concrete.

The frame for the basement and ground floor was substantially beam and column work. The superstructure frame was made up of columns and wide-span lattice trusses, reverting to beamwork for the plant rooms and roof.

Each floor level was decked with Ribdeck 60, the decking at the plant room and roof levels being perforated. There were five main staircases through the structure. The staircases were prefabricated in steel, and the landings and treads were concrete-filled on site after erection.

All of the structural steelwork was fabricated at Octavius Atkinson's production works in Harrogate, North Yorkshire, and transported to site as required by road.

The programme called for steel erection to be completed in 12 weeks and metal decking in 11 weeks, with completion one week after steel erection.

Erection characteristics

In common with many city sites, the area available for construction was limited to the footprint of the plan area of the finished building. The only access available for offloading of deliveries was from a lay-by gantry off Appold Street and for part of the time an access road which separated phase 5 construction and previously constructed phase 4.

The site was serviced by two tower cranes which between them gave hook coverage to the whole area.

Due to the access restrictions, together with the difficulties of working in the City and the tight programme, the superstructure steelwork and decking was predominantly delivered at night. Two shifts were operated, one day and one night shift, the main erection being carried out during the day, with the night shift principally offloading, preparing and dressing the steel for the next day's erection.

Great emphasis was placed on the steel being fabricated and delivered to site strictly in the sequence required by the erection teams. Delivery schedules were prepared by the site management and directed to the relevant tower crane.

Superstructure erection

The erection of the superstructure was sequential band by band in a vertically ascending order. The structure was divided into three longitudinal strips for erection sequencing. The central strip included the main services core to the structure.

The erection sequence was

(*a*) erect main services core followed by the remainder of the central strip

(*b*) overlapping in time, erect either or each of the outer strips

(*c*) erect temporary bracing.

The core and central strip were always in advance of the outer strips, leading to a stepped form of erection. This enabled the two tower cranes to work efficiently without interfering with each other and allowed for efficient phasing of the deck installation and handovers to following trades.

The main frame was designed for 'fast erection', comprising columns and wide-span lattice trusses with perimeter beamwork, although the perimeter moment connections proved to be very onerous. This was a result of the engineer requiring the moment connections generally to develop 80% of the full plastic moment capacity of beam, and led to 16 500 HSFG bolts being used, an average of thirty 30 mm dia. HSFG bolts in each connection.

The bolting and torquing up was a critical activity and the night shift was increased to boost production.

The overall philosophy was to have metal decking following behind frame erection by two levels, so that as each band was handed over for the following trades, one working level was handed over with the level above acting as a crash deck. In the event, with the three-strip principle adopted, an earlier handover was achieved to the lower-level deck to allow for reinforcing mesh/bar to be landed prior to the air space above being covered by the next level of deck.

Most of the steelwork was erected using the tower cranes provided. A small number of perimeter ground to second-floor level columns had to be erected by mobile cranes, and two 11 t girders at seventh-floor level had to be semi-propped during erection.

The erection sequence was followed largely uninterrupted until roof construction commenced. At this point, and at about the time when resources would have been reducing, a number of additional factors came into play which led to an increase of resource and prolongation of programme. The main entrance steelwork final information was late and led to additional work. The client's requirements for the basement were subject to late variations which led to substantial re-work on site. A number of items of additional work were instructed, leading to considerable additional site work; examples of this are

(a) window-washing-machine pedestals
(b) squash court and viewing gallery steelwork
(c) plant room steelwork to roof and basement
(d) additional service hole trimmers, mainly between seventh floor level and the roof
(e) variations/additions to lift-motor pit support structures.

In parallel with this, as its design and approval had run significantly over programme, the staircase required erection much later than anticipated, with all the attendant problems of other trade interface.

A number of activities still remained live at the end of the structural build, and this led Octavius Atkinson into areas of interface that had not originally existed, making life difficult for the teams in place. Considerable co-ordination was required to progress these works, while detailed programming was required to maintain progress to meet the client's requirements.

Client—trade contractor organization

The client's overall objectives were made clear in the scope of works in terms of the 'build and burrow' method and the major interfaces for handovers, these being the ground floor handover for burrow release, the metal decking handover to the concrete trade contractor, and the frame handover for curtain walling installation.

What was less clear was the interface with other trade contractors, such as those for fire-boarding/dry-lining, lift installation, roof-level weatherproofing, and services work.

Moreover, what was not made clear at all was the programme for

(*a*) the basement construction in its final form
(*b*) the additional items for miscellaneous plant — lifts, cooling-water towers, etc.
(*c*) the window-washing-machine pedestals
(*d*) the handrailing fixing (although it is accepted that many of the stair interface problems would not have existed had the stair design/approval and fabrication not been so significantly late).

The operation of the site process by the client's construction manager, Bovis—Schal, had many good points

(*a*) design team meetings
(*b*) weekly trade contractor site co-ordination meetings
(*c*) daily co-ordination site meetings
(*d*) 7.30 a.m. co-ordination meetings
(*e*) director meetings.

The weekly co-ordination meetings, involving the current trade contractors, Bovis—Schal and Skidmore, Owings & Merrill were generally most beneficial. Octavius Atkinson's involvement started approximately one month before the work started on site and gave quite a natural lead-in to the company's activities. However, these meetings eventually became unwieldy and too lengthy when too many contractors were involved. For the future the construction manager will group the trade contractors according to the interfaces, or have more than one meeting.

The daily meetings, which involved site personnel at General Foreman level, were useful and should have been more successful. The biggest failing was the lack of discipline in punctuality and timing: this was a guilt shared by all.

The directors' meetings were initially very dynamic, with the operations directors and/or the chief executives of the trade contractors being brought face to face to recognize and resolve problems being encountered by their counterparts. In time, these meetings too become unwieldy and lost their penetration. In addition, they would have been better held around midday, which would have allowed the actions to be placed with the site team while the adrenaline was still flowing. As it was, one slept on the matter and in many cases relayed the message by telephone the following day.

The 7.30 a.m. co-ordination meetings leading up to handover were enlightening. Octavius Atkinson would not ordinarily have been involved at this stage: its involvement was due to the additional work items referred to earlier. These were primarily 'action' meetings, held every two weeks, setting targets and knocking down hurdles.

The good and the bad

The good points of the work in phase 5 of the Broadgate complex were

(*a*) the intent with respect to co-ordination, and regular co-ordination meetings with the various elements of the on-site and off-site works

(*b*) the rewards for performance, such as site notices applauding record achievements, and the champagne awards and mentions at director meetings

(*c*) the profile put on safety, including signs, competitions and the constant monitoring.

The bad points were

(*a*) the time which was involved in resolving stair design and the end quality of product; this was a failure for all of the team — Bovis—Schal, Skidmore, Owings & Merrill, and Octavius Atkinson

(*b*) poor discipline with respect to attendances, punctuality, timing and continuity of meeting at all levels

(*c*) site team office accommodation; this could and should have been better

(*d*) initial welfare arrangements; this situation was redressed when Bovis—Schal set up and moved into the building, although belatedly at two thirds of the way through Octavius Atkinson's programme of works.

The following improvements could have been made, or could be made next time.

(*a*) There could have been earlier involvement in the contract with the design team.

(*b*) There could have been an earlier understanding of Skidmore, Owings & Merrill's way of working.

(*c*) A more comprehensive explanation could have been given at the time of the construction manager philosophy, with induction meetings at various levels.

(*d*) There could have been 'make it better meetings', like the Bovis—Schal 'wish lists' but involving trade contractors at all levels.

(*e*) A real commitment could have been made to sorting out the stairs, so that they could be truly erected with the structure — everybody was able to give the theory. I have not yet been on a project where the various teams have been able to do this, whether in Octavius Atkinson's own supply or supplied by others.

(*f*) The pressure and responsibility that Bovis—Schal exerted on its trade contractors for performance, particularly in respect to the co-ordination of activities with other trade contractors, led in itself to misunderstandings, disruption and hence a reduction in productivity. This was particularly relevant in the basement area, where it was left to all intents and purposes to a 'free for all'!

The contract and its risks

There has been much discussion in respect to the Broadgate contract terms and conditions, although Octavius Atkinson's view was that in real terms there were only three clauses which were more onerous than in other forms of contract.

First, trade contractors are deemed to have the expertise to include within their bids any and every refinement which the project team may make provided it is within the scope of works. This leaves them with the dilemma of pricing potential changes or additions, and in doing so possibly losing the contract, or taking the risk that the contract will be built exactly as described in the documents and drawings provided. Clearly the decision is a difficult one to make, and one that I believe is unreasonable and could well prove disadvantageous to both client and trade contractor.

Second, the contract allows the construction manager to make judgements prior to any ascertainment or agreement and to deduct monies from the trade contractor without any recourse to adjudication, an action which could very seriously affect one's cash flow. Here also the clauses do seem unreasonable.

Third, damages are at large (i.e. unlimited), which really needs no explanation!

Clearly one cannot price for such risks. In fairness, Octavius Atkinson's contract at Broadgate was without any such problem areas. The company took the view in submitting its bid that these conditions would only be applied in the event of its failing to perform, and it had total confidence in its own abilities.

The payment terms were most certainly attractive, giving payment four weeks after application, which included payment for black and fabricated steel off site. In addition, variations were valued and agreed 'up front' and again payment was prompt.

Final account negotiations were relatively straightforward and completed before the completion of the company's work. When agreement was reached, the full amount of retention was released.

Relationships

Octavius Atkinson's relationship with the client had been and has been particularly enlightening: in his 'open book' approach with substantial 'front line' involvement Rosehaugh Stanhope defused and short-circuited potential problem areas which could otherwise have involved long drawn out negotiations involving several key people over a significant period of time.

Octavius Atkinson has enjoyed a relationship which has seen it involved on a total of six contracts virtually continuously since the autumn of 1986, involving more than 12 000 t of structural steelwork. The long-term relationship has itself built for the company a trust and understanding of the client's objectives.

The company has been fortunate also in that its relationship with the construction manager has built up and been continuous over a period of four years. The company had difficulties earlier on in understanding the philosophies of construction management, which in truth it felt were not always totally understood by the construction manager's team either. As time went on, however, I like to think that each developed an excellent understanding of the other's operations, particularly at Construction Director level.

There were times, probably due mainly to the sheer size of the Broadgate project, that the project management became too bureaucratic and administration-orientated. This certainly had its frustrations and is an area which I believe could be improved.

The company had to work extremely hard at forming a relationship and understanding with the architect/structural engineer, particularly on the phase 5 project.

It has, however, formed the view that the quality of information received from them was of a particularly high standard, and once Octavius Atkinson learnt an appreciation of how their system operated it never really had problems at the front end (i.e. in the preparation and approval of fabrication drawings) and believes it formed a first-class working relationship with them.

It did, however, find their handling of their Inspection Authority clumsy, to a large degree inefficient and without any real understanding of 'fitness for purpose'. This was an area that at times provoked enormous emotion over issues which could have been, and generally were, settled relatively easily by a sound engineering approach.

Benefits of construction management
Octavius Atkinson's involvement at Broadgate introduced the company to construction management and it benefited in a number of ways.

Construction management gave the company clear responsibilities and it was accepted as an experienced and competent trade contractor, rid of the 'subcontractor' image.

The company was encouraged to have an open relationship with the client, which itself developed a two-way understanding of problems and the formation of a commercial trust.

The 'can do' attitude which existed throughout the team was refreshing and proved a motivating force on its own. It encouraged progressing the work as a priority over establishing the claim.

The company felt very much part of the team. It was involved in many of the discussions, which resulted in its being more committed to the objectives.

Most significantly of all, construction management changed the company's attitude and approach to construction: it wakened the senses of those of us who were involved to the overall objective rather than the parochial view, and as we achieved each target we grew in confidence and set our aims even higher.

The view of a dry-lining trade contractor

W. A. BROWNE, Managing Director, W. A. Browne Building Services Ltd

The business of W. A. Browne is split 50:50 between private housing in the north-east of England and fast-build contracts in London, where our client is a member of the Stanhope Group of companies. Browne's only sphere of activity is installing dry-wall. This scope of activity came about as a result of an introduction from British Gypsum to Stanhope Properties. Right from my initial meeting with Ian Macpherson, representing Bovis—Schal and Peter Rogers, representing Stanhope, there was a feeling of openness, a willingness to exchange ideas, with no predetermined historical rules to play the game by. This allowed Brownes to embark on the introduction of new systems and operations affecting the way in which dry-wall is installed, building on ideas seen in North

America and also some systems that the company had managed to adopt in its operation in the north-east of England. The company was given every opportunity by the client to learn from his experiences of earlier failures on other projects. This gave Brownes the stimulation and encouragement to go forward and to respond with a new method statement for the operation of dry-wall on fast-build contracts.

How can improvements be made on the method of material handling? Larger hoists are needed, capable of taking up larger plasterboard sizes packed in more than 1 t lifts. Metal studs, because of the floor heights in today's buildings, need to be in a continuous run: these are not able to go into the hoists at present available. Why has it taken so long to establish that the effective management of materials requires larger hoisting facilities? This question is now being addressed and will no doubt lead to phase 2 of Brownes' logistical attitude being adopted.

Logistics, good planning of materials, is a key to a good project. In a JCT situation trade contractors would not normally be consulted about such matters as logistics. My first observation therefore on the difference between JCT and construction management concerns the early discussion focusing on the client's objectives and the trade contractors' solutions to the problems posed by these objectives — rather than a bill of quantities, with specialist contractors having no part in the compilation of documentation that they are being asked to price.

Having established that now material is on site in a fit manner in which to use, Brownes adopt an attitude of good quality management on site, with a properly trained workforce, stimulated once again by the client and construction manager, who is seen to be involved and is willing to provide awards for achievement (i.e. prizes for safety; for the fastest, tidiest, trade contractor), and the encouragement to participate in the project as an overall entity. Brownes issued each of their operatives with a pair of overalls with the company name and the project on the back, and T shirts, similarly embossed, for their summer use.

Why ...?

Why has it taken so long, and still does take so long, for this message of stimulation to get across the full construction management/client/trade contractors team? There seems to be dilution of the concepts down through the workforce. For instance, some trade contractors are still operating as subcontractors: is it because they are not aware of the difference, not aware of what their responsibilities are, or are they too used to doing things in the 'old traditional' way? Brownes' ability to perform was further enhanced by the relationships between the client, British Gypsum and themselves, and by British Gypsum's agreement as a material supplier to adopt a new and modern approach to the way in which material was packaged and handled, and to assist in a hands-on manner which contributed to the successful installation of the dry lining. Such willingness establishes confidence with the architect, confidence with the client and the construction management team; it enables greater productivity and vastly enhanced standards of quality to be achieved.

Why is it that trade contractors still want to adopt the subcontracting attitude of not being open, 'cards on table' if they have a problem? Why not bring that problem to the table? The alternative — telling the construction manager what he wants to hear in a hope that the problem will go away — only leads to frustration and further discussions at a later date, and the problems still requiring a solution on the table. Tell the truth and re-programme to suit what is actually going to happen — not what you want somebody to think is going to happen.

Problem-solving at the work face, a 'hands on' approach, has been adopted, where the client, the construction manager, the architect and the trade contractor all have a hand and a responsibility in the way in which a problem is recognized and overcome. This does require a basic honesty in an approach to a job, and traditional attitudes of 'it's not my job, it's not my problem' have got to be avoided. Why is it that communication seems to take so long to get passed down the line? One of the greatest advancements achieved through the use of construction management is the way in which the planning and programming of works and work areas is dealt with.

Clear access routes throughout each floor of the building show exactly where materials shall or shall not be stored and where routes to move materials are available. Clearly defined work areas, clearly programmed, give trade contractors free use of a designated area for a period of time. But here again the message does seem to be getting diluted, and there are problems in trying to convert the uninitiated to this system of operation, which if followed properly can only help in speed, quality and lack of waste. From Brownes' point of view, plasterboard should be taken into the building once, it should be used in a good quality to a correct standard with a quality assurance/quality control during the course of construction, and the very minimum of waste should be taken out of the site — there should not (as seems to be the standard at the moment) be as much plasterboard going out the building as goes into the building.

Moving on

It is the truth that in $3\frac{1}{2}$ years of contractural liaison between myself and my client we have had no cause at any stage to refer to the contract, to either make a point or back up an argument. My company is paid directly by the client, with no involvement from the construction manager (other than his advice to the client on the financial status of our account). In this way the client knows when he is getting value for money, and has the ability to control his purse strings at first hand. This does appear to be the one basic element of construction management that is difficult for a standard subcontractor to understand. The fact that if a company chooses its client correctly and establishes his ability to pay, if it does him a good contract and does the work to a correct standard, it will end up getting what is due to it. It is a two-way passage of information and relationships — a mutual benefit arrangement. How can this now be enhanced? As we at Brownes have learnt our lessons over the past few years, we are now demanding that we have a better awareness of the client's future workload: as the problem of skilled resources becomes greater within the industry and management is still difficult to obtain, it is of great help to be able to plan ahead so as to obtain continuity.

Continuity for the client, construction management and trade contractors will eventually lead to the perfect project: construction managers will be doing what they are paid for, and that is more of a co-ordinating role — they will not have to tell trade contractors when to go and do their operation and where to go and do it — the trade contractors will manage themselves, and the client will walk round and say how pleased he is. All of his observations will have been taken on board. The client, the construction manager and the trade contractors will all be proud of what they produce, and will actually create more profit internally within their own organizations.

Roles

We at Brownes see our role as a trade contractor within the relationships as being just as important as that of the architect and the construction manager, and have learnt to be very positive about how we express ourselves: we make our views known, heard and listened to.

The traditional main contractor views specialist sub-trades always as the poor relation: well I, for one, will no longer tolerate this situation.

Why is it that even now construction managers, when it is they that are being criticized for either the level of their management or the way in which their management is conducting itself, retreat back into the stance of a traditional main contractor/subcontractor relationship? For instance, when a trade contractor levels criticism at a construction management company about the quality of the people it has on site, this is taken as a direct insult and a subject that should not be voiced by the trade contractor; but it seems to be fair game for a construction manager to continually criticize a trade contractor and demand changes in its management. (More resource is the cry.) We at Brownes are learning to adopt the attitude that if something is not right it needs bringing to the table, and it is incumbent on all parties to view it in the correct manner and to take observations on board: the client is our employer, not the construction manager. The construction manager is a member of the team, a very important part of the operation, but he is a tool used by the client to obtain a building.

The future

We at Brownes have great difficulty now when asked to operate under a standard JCT form of contract, which puts us into a position of being a subcontractor, with no direct relationship with either the architect or the client: we find that this has a stifling effect on our organization and actually means that it can take longer to get problems solved, it takes longer to get our ideas across and probably ends up with a building that has cost more to dry-wall than it ever should have done.

Hopefully in the future there will be

(*a*) more professional trade contractors
(*b*) better induction of all parties to a new project
(*c*) even greater emphasis on logistics
(*d*) even earlier design input by trade contractors.

Broadgate opened a new concept, but also posed a few as yet unanswered questions.

The view of a building services trade contractor

R. M. MARGRAVE, Operations Director, Rosser & Russell

Rosser & Russell Building Services is 100 years old and has an annual turnover of £60 million. It operates principally in London and the South East and is accredited with BS 5750 Part 1 quality assurance. The company has executed many fast-build projects during the past ten years, with values ranging from £1.5 million to £10 million. The fastest was a fit-out project at the Broadgate development, for Shearson Lehman, where £7 million of services were installed, commissioned and handed over during a continuous 16 week period.

Two major phases of the Broadgate development have been selected to exemplify the principles of fast-track building services installation: the shell and core elements for phase 5 and phases 9 and 10. These two contracts, although neighbouring projects on the same development, had widely diverse ingredients in the management and professional team make-up and philosophies. They make an interesting comparison.

Normally the building services contractor has the unenviable role of a low-profile cog in the hierarchial wheel. This is somewhat disappointing considering the value of his work, its degree of difficulty, (often made worse by circumstances beyond his control), the retention or acquisition of good staff, and the potential risk arising from onerous conditions of contract.

Some views in this paper may seem provocative to construction managers and professional team members. They are meant to be so, and in the subsequent sections, sound contractual and technical opinions are offered as an answer to some of the encumbrances placed on all concerned. It is hoped that all parties can learn from these opinions to the overall benefit of future projects. Broadgate has had the effect of raising the status of the building services trade contractor to where, certainly in the eyes of that client, his standing is equal to that of others.

Role, objective and risks

Rosser & Russell Building Services was appointed to contract the design, development and installation of the mechanical and plumbing services, including associated plant; set to work; commission; prove and hand over.

The phase 5 building was of steel-frame construction, while phases 9 and 10 were built using traditional concrete methods. The two differing structures did not present any change in Rosser & Russell's approach, or attitude, albeit the later project was double in size and value. The building services followed the same design principles, although in external appearance and layout the buildings were totally different.

The major objective of Rosser & Russell was to achieve a quality installation — within budget, and in accordance with the schedule. This involved a competitive price and taking commercial views on the contractual risks. 'Do you price all prelim items, and at what cost? (Or, 'What can you ignore?') This is all very risky. It is a well known fact in building services that, 'He who leaves something out, wins the job'.

The Broadgate experience

Broadgate is about new techniques, innovations, and achieving objectives. These are all actively encouraged by the client. Cash prizes for good ideas are welcomed by both the company and operatives alike.

Rosser & Russell were greatly helped to improve their efficiency on both phase 5 and phases 9 and 10 by being afforded good access to the building, clear access to plant locations for material movement, and use of the tower cranes. Such facilities have been difficult to obtain on other projects outside Broadgate, as few management contractors or construction managers believe that service trades have an equal right for crane use, and clear access ways to work areas. Perhaps they could learn from the Broadgate experience.

Pre-construction lead-in times are significant in fast-build projects. For phase 5 the lead time was short whereas for phases 9 and 10 it was reasonable, allowing more emphasis to be put on off-site prefabrication techniques for the latter project. Early in the contract Rosser & Russell realized that good access and clean work areas minimize risks and improve efficiency. Unfortunately the old chestnut of 'schedule control' arose, whereby nobody in the construction management team was detailed, or wanted, to monitor thoroughly all the trade contractors to ensure that they kept to the programme and completed fully all their tasks at each work face.

This, Rosser & Russell are convinced, is the reason for the panics that occurred near project completion and increased damage to installed services. The company's complaints were met by the 'protection to practical completion' cry from the construction manager, and it was left with the problem.

However, at Broadgate the client, with his active participation throughout the project, reacted fairly and paid towards the cost of repair. Rosser & Russell believe that had the construction manager dealt more effectively with planning interfaces then this damage would not have occurred, or at least it would have been drastically reduced. Shell and core works are basic and simple, but are made more difficult by the damage problem, often resulting in crippling repair costs. Poor co-ordination procedures in a multi-trade package system also have adverse effects.

Reimbursement for these costs certainly had an impact on the company's approach for tendering for phases 9 and 10. It did not include for damage, even though the protection clause was still in the document. It was the trade contractor's risk again.

The team

Broadgate has also promoted teamwork at all levels from the client downwards, and the attitude of the 'can do' approach has undoubtedly rubbed off on many of the contractors who have been involved. Rosser & Russell see the contrary to this on other projects, where the company works alongside contractors (some of whom are in its own industry) who have not operated at Broadgate. Their approach is the old way, slow, laborious and 'that's the way it's always been done'. There is not much change there.

The company tries to instil in its subcontractors, and others it works with, that the can do approach is best. It is a struggle, but there are increased financial rewards, and that's what it's all about: profit.

Rosser & Russell's role within the team was to take the lead in services co-ordination, even though other services trade contractors, such as electrical, ductwork, controls and insulation, were appointed directly by the client under separate trade contracts. The company knows that mechanical contractors, who have extensive knowledge of all associated building services trades, are best suited to this task, provided of course that they are paid for it.

However, the company believes that the multi-service package system is wrong, and that mechanical and electrical should be at best a single contract, or at worst let as two separate individual packages. This is a constant argument, and one the company had at Broadgate with the professional and construction teams, who said that multi-package projects were cheaper, and provided a better financial deal for the clients. The company does not believe this, and as yet nobody has provided substantial evidence for it. The company knows the problems, and the losses it is caused by the system, especially when the calibre of the construction management staff is not the best. These signs were seen at Broadgate, where the team for phases 9 and 10 was far superior to that on phase 5. The company is of the opinion that this is one reason why it achieved better efficiency and greater profit on phases 9 and 10.

The good participation by the client at Broadgate has instilled considerable confidence in the company, in that the client takes an active part in problem-solving, and sometimes intervenes, with a commonsense approach, to 'overrule' a contractual stance taken by its professional and construction team. Phase 5 had its fair share of problems, and the way the client reacted helped in the company's deliberations when settling the final tender figure for phases 9 and 10.

The upper managers of the construction management team were strong, and always coerced contractors to get on with it — nothing is impossible! Very often they were most vociferous. The site management, however, tended to avoid problems and shelter behind the contract. The site management on phase 5 was poor, possibly due to the many changes in personnel throughout the contract; on phases 9 and 10 it was notably better. But on both projects it needed to take a more active role in programming and problem-solving.

The company's biggest problems were associated with the building services design, which was undertaken by American consultants and produced to American standards. The company's criticism is not made to enhance the status of their British counterparts (heaven knows, some of these are very poor), but certain points must be taken on board for the future. The problems listed in Table 1 contributed to frustrations and poor financial results on phase 5, but this experience helped the company in its approach to tendering for phases 9 and 10.

Not all was doom and gloom. The submission and approval process, when understood, promotes planning and the analysis of manufacturers' quotations and literature more closely, as they are checked thoroughly by the consultants. All associated documentation and data for each item must be provided at this stage.

This process highlights potential problems with equipment at the pre-manufacture phase and gives time for correction. Having this information available at an early stage enables the production of clash-free co-ordination drawings, thus increasing the speed of installation.

Relationships

Relationships were very important. Excellent rapport was built with the client: because the client was always fair and reasonable the trust built up, allowing the contractor to take risks, with knowledge that at the end of the day he would be treated fairly. Both projects had their problems, but on other developments similar situations would have probably ended in contractual disputes. At Broadgate the company's contract has always remained 'in the drawer'. This is where 'construction management with client' wins hands down over other forms of contract.

It was difficult to build good relationships with the construction

Table 1. Problems experienced by Rosser & Russell with building services design

The pre-designed service layouts were lacking in detail when compared with the standards the company normally expects to receive at tender stage; much of the work was design outline, and in the company's opinion far from complete.

The company's interpretation of the missing information on the drawings at tender stage also contributed to poor profitability, and drastically increased its draughting costs against those estimated.

Approval of drawings took too long on phase 5, which did not help the short pre-construction period; although it was reduced for phases 9 and 10, it still took too long. (This should attract a delay penalty paid for by those making the approval.)

The information required on working drawings was far greater under the American system. On phase 5 the company underestimated this because it was not clear at tender stage, but made allowances for phases 9 and 10.

The specification was American and very open-ended. Substantial errors were made in pricing and obtaining quotations and manufacturers' literature to put forward during the submission and approval process on phase 5 — a point the company rectified on phases 9 and 10, having learnt another painful lesson. This resulted in considerable loss of pre-construction time, because much of the submission was rejected, and had to be reworked.

For phases 9 and 10 the company was aware of the pitfalls and responded accordingly, but was annoyed to find that the specification, when issued, was still based on American standards, and that its earlier comments, criticisms and requests for the specification to become Anglicized had not been respected.

During post-tender interviews it was stressed that the company must provide decision-makers to head its site teams. It did — unlike the consulting engineer's team, who often had to refer matters back to head office, and sometimes to the USA. But the Site Engineer did try hard to beat the system in the interest of the project.

management staff on phase 5 due to the changes in personnel. The company did get the impression, however, that the services contractors were the 'poor relations', and that at site level it was difficult to obtain a fair hearing.

Phases 9 and 10 were different: relationships were established early, the construction management staff remained throughout the project, and the engineering imput was of a higher quality. (An ex-services contractor was in charge!)

The works

Broadgate brought Rosser & Russell many good attitudes which have been put to advantage on other projects. Cleaner floors and the constant removal of rubbish allowed more efficiency, and the use of more advanced plant or equipment to aid installation. Operative labour liked working there, after the learning curve was overcome. Good bonuses were achieved because of the good working environment. Good site accommodation was provided, and the client's 'celebrations' at appropriate intervals helped with enthusiasm. Phases 9 and 10 commenced as phase 5 was finished, so there was continuity of work for the same operatives, who were by then indoctrinated with can-do.

The major frustration for the operatives proved to be the number of times they returned to areas to repair damage.

If the company could improve or change things, it would insist that the construction management team devoted more time to getting involved on site with trade contractors to monitor and control, rather than leave it to the trade contractors themselves. This would avoid the last-minute panics, and many returns to uncompleted work faces. Construction managers tend to rely on meetings, which are too frequent and involve too many people to be productive and instructive. Short sharp meetings with each specialist, monitoring the discussions and checking on site are the answer. This will allow the 'action men' of the trade contractors to get on with their work. More direct involvement by the contract managers would reduce the panics, and sudden increases in labour that the trade contractors are expected to cope with at the drop of a hat. A trade contractor cannot 'open another box of men', nor can it disrupt other contracts to suit.

There are two points which the company regards as having had a detrimental effect on its performance, and which will be object lessons for the future. First, the metal decking used on phase 5 went out of shape under concrete loading, creating problems with the insert fixings for pipe supports: many just fell out. Was this the result of a short cut in quality to obtain a cheap price on the package? It cost Rosser & Russell time and money to overcome.

Second, phases 9 and 10, being a traditional concrete structure, created problems in that fast large-scale pouring had to be achieved to meet the programme. Although records were set, severe problems were often encountered with finished levels, and many holes were missing. Again, delays were caused to the company's works, and additional cost.

Fast-build specialists

To make improvements for the end user, the company believes that fast build requires a specialist team of service engineers who understand the client's needs, and who are constantly working in this environment. They think faster and anticipate problems before they occur: they have a greater awareness of movement trends in the subcontract market, together with manufacturers'/suppliers' ability to perform in any given period. This is promoted by establishing contacts, and building relationships at the highest level. Certainly not all service engineers are suited to this environment, and companies must select their teams carefully before embarking on such projects.

Commercial aspects

Profit margins within the building services industry are poor, and show little sign of improving. Therefore companies must home in on projects that will give them their required profit. Construction management contracts, operated properly, are the answer, especially when one looks at the onerous clauses for payment to contractors under JCT and management contracts.

Cash flow and profit are paramount, especially when an excellent service and a quality installation are provided. Payments have always been good, regular, and fair at Broadgate. With constant client involvement at all stages throughout the project, and an 'open door' policy, the client is aware of the problems and listens to the trade contractors. Payments are made direct, and therefore not tampered with by management or general contractors.

The company can state instances where payments were made between valuation periods when special circumstances prevailed. These were made after direct discussion with the client, who listened, evaluated and made a judgement accordingly. This attitude instils confidence and provides the necessary carrot to achieve even better results.

This paper has covered some of the estimating pitfalls of phase 5. The company priced/evaluated the risk on phases 9 and 10 accordingly. The final result was very much better than for the preceding contract, which was taken at a very tight commercial and competitive basis, being the first building on the second phase of Broadgate.

Being treated fairly by the client on 'contentious' issues at phase 5, without having to revert to the contract, gave reassurance in the tendering process for phases 9 and 10. The learning curve had been overcome, site conditions were improving, relationships with all parties were established, and some were improving. All of this had a bearing on the company's pricing structure. However, the company is convinced that it was only treated fairly because of its performance during the contract. It is sure that failure to perform and meet all of the targets set would have resulted in the client adopting a totally different attitude, and maybe the contract would have 'come out of the drawer'.

Conclusion

Rosser & Russell have benefited from Broadgate projects, as have many other trade contractors. The company believes that its business approach and commercial acumen has enhanced its status in the eyes of the industry.

The building services installation is always foremost in the occupier's mind, long after the structural engineer has stopped worrying about his stress calculations: faults with the services are only obscured by earth tremors.

The company's relationship with all parties has blossomed, and it is being considered for future projects with the same teams. Repeat business is the best business. The company hopes that this will continue, and will go out of its way to ensure that it does.

Broadgate, London: phase 8

The view of a cladding trade contractor

M. L. PELHAM, Group Managing Director, Conder Group plc

Elemeta — the largest of the three cladding activities of the Conder Group — has its fourth contract at Broadgate on phase 8: this contract is for $16\,000\,\text{m}^2$ of panellized cladding. An earlier contract on phase 5 was similar but of a less complex nature, and on phases 9 and 10 Elemeta designed, supplied and erected the atria.

The cladding on phase 8 is made up of 1055 panels, of which there are 600 different types with a maximum repeat of any one type of 45. For the most part these panels have to be erected in particular sequences linked to the nature of their design; the developer's marketing requirements and the fit-out activities which follow on have to be taken into account also.

The cladding trade contractor, with the lift supplier, has the distinction of supplying one of the longest lead procurement items, although he does not come on to site until late in the construction progress. As one of the last to arrive on site he has to accept the tolerances of the building 'as built' and may be faced with re-sequencing his activities to take into account the progress of other subcontractors, the developer's marketing requirements, or particular fit-out issues.

Unlike most other trades the cladding trade contractor has a large off-site design and manufacturing operation which gives him a high fixed overhead.

Compared with all the other specialist subcontracting activities in the Conder Group, such as steel structures building services, pods, and stick and column curtain walling, Elemeta's panellized cladding activities have by far the highest level of off-site fixed cost.

Forms of contract

None of the existing forms of contract reflects the true economics of the bespoke panellized cladding trade contractor. Wisely, the employer and his management team involve Elemeta at the very inception of the project, often before planning permission has been obtained. The employer is understandably desirous of reserving capacity for his project and will approach Elemeta with his initial requirements prior to detailed planning application and certainly before the start of detailed design. Elemeta then become involved in what is to them the first stage, the 'conceptual' design, during which they develop and agree a technical approach and solution to the architect's requirements. At that stage the outside envelope of the building may well look deceptively simple and repetitive and the programme will show a logical, plausible sequence of work.

Several, often many, months later, when the employer has grappled with detailed planning requirements, possession of the site (for example the pub on the corner of phase 8 at Broadgate) and the design input from other trade contractors, the reality is that the cladding is no longer repetitive or simple. Hence 600 of the 1055 panels on phase 8 are different.

The cladding trade contractor is expected to regard this as normal, and to accommodate the changes into his design and manufacturing programme. At the same time as the time-scale of the project varies he is expected to keep detailed design and manufacturing capacity available, an overhead that, if not working, may be costing as much as £1 million per quarter.

Against this background I believe that all of the existing forms of contract fail to address the problems of a trade contractor who is also a bespoke manufacturer and who is expected to maintain a large detailed design force and highly skilled workforce available whose workload has to be tailored to programme requirements that only emerge in the second half of the site construction period. The form of the trade contract at Broadgate further adds to his concerns, with the 'damages at large' risk.

I would suggest that a more appropriate form of contract would be as follows

(a) a design fee to cover the initial development of the design and the agreement of the technical solution with the architect

(b) a 'detail and manufacture' price, made up in two parts: a fixed monthly charge commencing on the date on which the trade contractor contracts to commit his detailing and manufacturing capacity to the project; and a variable charge based on factory output, covering materials, productive labour etc.

(c) a site erection cost based on a scheduled start date and phased release of sections of the works by the employer to the trade contractor.

This arrangement still leaves the trade contractor fully at risk for his own performance but does more accurately reflect the underlying economics of the relationship between the trade contractor and the employer, leading to a fairer apportionment of risk and ultimately a lower cost to the employer.

Design office and factory organization

Design and build of cladding to a fast-build schedule is a process requiring a strong project management team. It differs from fast-build construction only in the respect that the main centre of activity has changed its location from site to factory.

The trade contractors detailed design and manufacturing programme has to reconcile four conflicting requirements

(a) the availability of precise detailed information from the architect

(b) the logical design sequence of the cladding itself

(c) the desirability of attempting to batch similar sub-components through the manufacturing capacity

(d) the overriding priority of site erection sequence, which is dictated partly by the physical logic of the cladding system and partly by the requirements of the employer or the actual conditions encountered on site relative to the work of other parties.

Successful management of the programme requires an absolute acceptance that the requirements of the project must always be dominant compared with those of either design office or factory:

the construction sequence must drive other activities, from design, through materials procurement and component manufacture to final assembly.

Design and engineering to a strict and ordered schedule does not come too easily to the majority of people engaged in this sort of task. Fast-build cladding projects do, however, require that design is completed in sequence and on time without slippage. A day lost in progress at this stage must be treated as seriously as one in the later manufacturing and installation phases — the adverse effect is comparable.

The quality and accuracy of drawings and production information are fundamental to fast build. Drawings must be produced to suit the user, not the design office. A production worker or supervisor needs the relevant information displayed on one or two drawings, rather than having to continually refer to other documents for details.

Checking of drawing before issue is crucial and calls for mature experience and strong commitment by senior personnel. Errors must be eliminated at this stage before the manufacture and assembly processes are affected. Prefabrication off site inevitably means that where design draughting or manufacturing errors have slipped through the quality check and a defective panel has arrived on site, it almost certainly will have to return to the factory for modification.

Planning and controlling the construction sequence

The erection sequence on a project is liable to change through the course of the project for a number of reasons. These may include weather, material availability, manufacturing progress, interface with other contractors, or employer's requirements for marketing to tenants. At Elemeta a control system has therefore been adopted which is designed to cope with a constantly changing and developing situation.

The hub of the system is a 'control room' through which all information relative to design, manufacture and erection of panels is routed. By ensuring that the status of each aspect of the process to produce an installed panel is recorded in the control room on a daily basis, it is possible to optimize production and ensure that critical parts of the construction sequence are completed to programme. Although simple in concept the system has two significant advantages.

(*a*) It is dynamic and updated on a daily basis.
(*b*) The board gives a pictorial representation of progress and highlights the need for action to maintain the erection sequence and schedule.

All panels and kits of components in the factory are marked with distinctive labels showing panel and erection sequence numbers corresponding with those on the control board. If the erection sequence can be changed advantageously, labels and cards are immediately revised.

Materials management

The effective use of factory and storage space dictates the need to adopt a just-in-time supply system for materials. Just-in-time is determined by the period required to sort and then allocate to specific panels the necessary components. With an allowance for some component replacement and changes in construction sequence, material is generally not required at the factory more than three weeks ahead of manufacture.

Two particular features of the materials management systems at Elemeta deserve mention. The first is the unique numbering of all components by magnetic bar coding as used in a department store: tracking of components through all stages of manufacturing and assembly is thereby easily effected. The second feature is the concept of component marshalling for groups of panels at the earliest possible stage to ensure the availability of the materials to maintain a smooth production flow.

Handling and fixing of cladding panels

Maintenance of a fast-build programme on site on phase 8 depends to a large extent on the effective use of tower cranes and the development wherever possible of alternative methods of lifting and fixing.

Some storage for panels at site is considered essential, and this was arranged on the roof. Site storage enables the operation of transporting large panels into central London to be divorced from lifting and fixing, thus improving the smooth flow of erection of the panels.

Storage at ground level, though of course severely restricted, is particularly important in the sort of stormy weather conditions experienced. Offloading arrangements which are independent of tower crane availability must be considered in greater depth for future projects.

Fast build

The attitudes engendered by a particular form of contract are crucial to the success of a cladding project, given the complexity of panellized bespoke curtain walling, its long lead time, the high fixed costs of the trade contractor, and the sheer volume of often changing detail in the external envelope of the building. For these reasons the JCT lump sum and many of the management contracting forms of contract do not seem appropriate in that they are often of an 'adversarial' nature.

The factor which is crucial to the success of providing a complex, highly detailed product is first-class communications between the employer, his design team and his construction managers.

Other than certain aspects of the form of contract itself, I believe that the arrangements at Broadgate have created a favourable climate — albeit, as yet, far from perfect. The emphasis on teamwork, directors' meetings, communications, the general ethos of recognizing achievement and excellence, all build a positive atmosphere within the 'working team'.

However, would this not be greatly reinforced if the 'working team' participated in the development profits in proportion to the extent that they are required to carry its losses through the 'damages at large' clauses? Would this not be the ultimate demonstration by the employer of his commitment to the 'teamwork' principle that is essential to fast-building?